Hellbent for Paradise

Road Dog Publications was formed in 2010 as an imprint of Lost Classics Book Company and is dedicated to publishing the best in books on motorcycling and adventure travel. Visit us at www.roaddogpub.com.

Photographs on pages 198 & 215 courtesy of Kevin Kingham

Book cover design by Scarlett Rickard

ISBN 978-1-890623-70-8
Library of Congress Control Number: 2019936043

An Imprint of Lost Classics Book Company
This book also available in eBook format at online booksellers. ISBN 978-1-890623-71-5

Hellbent for Paradise

Tales from Aotearoa;
Land of the Long White Cloud

by

Zoë Cano

Publisher
Lake Wales, Florida

"All my life I've wanted to do something big,
something bigger and better than all the other jokers"

Burt Munro

About the Author

Zoë Cano, whose first name means "Life," is an adventurous traveller, writer, and photographer.

Born in Hereford, England, in the 1960s she moved to live and work in Paris for ten years before working in New York and finally, Boston, with extended periods in Brazil and Asia for the international events and exhibition business.

Zoë started rowing competitively and took the challenge to skiff the entire length of the Thames from its source in the centre of England to Greenwich. She has crossed the Peruvian Andes on horseback, motorcycled numerous times solo around the American continent, as well as this recent journey to the Antipodes.

Zoë lives in London and is also the author of the highly successful travel trilogy *Bonneville Go or Bust* (2013), *Southern Escapades* (2015), and *Chilli, Skulls & Tequila* (2017).

For more information on Zoë Cano, her books, and travels visit www.zoecano.com

Also by Zoë Cano

Bonneville Go or Bust—On the Roads Less Travelled

Southern Escapades

Chilli, Skulls & Tequila—Notes from Baja California

CONTENTS

Hellbent for Paradise

PROLOGUE

2017. Exmoor. South England. August.

The bats were circling and dive bombing in the ever-darkening warm twilight sky as we walked from the old Somerset cottage, across the knee-high grass fields, along the gurgling stream, and up into the moors. It wasn't daytime, neither was it quite night time, but the first stars were already peeping out. Strange alien noises could be heard. A long harsh scream came from a nearby outbuilding, only to be reassured it was just a barn owl. We were deep into summer, and I was staying with my best friend Lulu and her brothers. We'd decided to go star gazing up in the Exmoor National Park, Europe's first International Dark Sky Reserve. So with blankets, bottles of wine, and torches in hand we marched the 355 metres to the top of Haddon Hill. In the ever-growing darkness, but under clear skies, we fumbled around to find a couple of grassy bunkers surrounded by heather and gorse to lie down in and shelter us from the cold wind.

It was now pitch dark. The boys tripped, laughing into one bunker, while Lulu and I, wrapped in blankets, lay in the other one looking up speechless into the limitless night sky. All was peacefully quiet, besides some remote Exmoor ponies neighing out into the distance.

Lulu unscrewed the bottle and took a generous swig before handing it to me. "So Zoë, what's happening? How's your summer been? It seems ages since we've had a good chin-wag."

I also take a gulp. "Biking up and down the country most weekends to festivals for the books."

Lulu nods in a boring way like that wasn't the sort of captivating answer she was looking for. "Ah ha. But more to the point, how's the planning going for the next big road trip? Under these stars we've got plenty of time to chat. Hey, look over there, the North Star and that ever-brightening and glowing white river of lights! That's our Milky Way."

I sigh in deep thought, looking up, "Well you know, I wanted to get to a place that I feel is as far away as possible from the UK but with interesting diversity. Funny, but it was when you'd spoken about your year off backpacking and spending unforgettable months in New Zealand twelve years ago that I thought, 'Yea I can play that one.' So out of curiosity, I started digging up stuff at the beginning of the year. For going that far I needed a decent amount of time, so with the quiet season in our winter, I blocked out the first three months next year and spontaneously booked the flights last January, just to get the dates I wanted!"

"Wow! Yea I know dates for flights down to New Zealand and Australia in our winter and their summer Christmas and New Year holiday season are manic."

Taking another swig of wine and waiting to see a shooting star fly over, I continue, "and then things have kind of snow-balled in a weird way, giving me strangely even stronger links to New Zealand that I never even knew existed. My cousin, Lois, researches our family tree. You're never going to believe this, but my great great granddad, Samuel Jacob Moses, was the first Jewish Justice of the Peace—a sort of magistrate—in Australia and New Zealand. He was also . . . " I stop and think about how I'm going to word it " . . . the Mohel. You know, the person who performs circumcisions! Records show that Samuel was the first, and for a long time, the only Jew in Australia and New Zealand authorized to perform that, so he travelled extensively just for that job! It's quite a story. He moved from London to Hobart, the capital of Tasmania, then known as Van Diemen's Land, in 1841. And with his brother-in-law, Louis Nathan, they ran a shipping and import-export merchants company in Hobart. Over the years, with their ships they exported wool to Britain and shipped countless necessary products to the new colonies of New Zealand, Victoria, and South Australia. Both Samuel and Nathan were also intrinsic in helping to fund the construction of the synagogue in Hobart, one of the first in Australasia. In 1859 he returned back to London with his wife, and a little later in 1873, was the first person to be buried in the new Willesden Jewish Cemetery in north London."

I lie back, feeling the cool breeze brush my face.

"You gotta be kidding! All your family going through the generations really were the travellers and pioneers of their time: your dad, your granddad, your great-great granddad, and now you."

Stop! But get this. There's even more bizarre serendipity with New Zealand. Just the other day I was walking into town through my local church and strangely for the first time saw this massive memorial for New Zealand soldiers in World War I. Why would this be in Walton-on-Thames? I guess my senses were even more alert as I then walked past our local pub, "The Wellington," formerly known as The Kiwi, and down through New Zealand Avenue! And my questions were answered pretty quickly, as there was a local event displaying The Mount Felix Tapestry—rows of finely needled tapestries depicting stories of the 27,000 wounded New Zealand soldiers who were taken in at the Mount Felix Hospital here in Walton-on-Thames during the First World War.

In fact, the first soldiers from Gallipoli arrived within days of the hospital opening. In July 1916, the New Zealand sick and wounded at Mount Felix numbered ninety officers and 2,352 other ranks, with 200 arriving every week from the battlefields. An anonymous medical man who attended the first train bringing wounded soldiers from the Somme in the middle of night in September 1916 recounted what he saw—"At 2.45AM the train pulled in to Walton Station. In five minutes the waiting room was filled to overflowing with our wounded. I looked at these worn, begrimed, travel-stained men and marvelled. I was looking—looking for something I couldn't find—for the buoyant, saucy, irrepressible cheerfulness . . . These men seemed almost strangers. They were so silent, so grim; one felt they had come from the very depths of Hell." Each of the ninety-five men on the train were given cocoa and cigarettes. As the conflict wore on, the people of Walton opened a canteen and handed out warm drinks and food to the wounded as they arrived in town. By October there were 4,740 wounded New Zealanders at the hospital. The convalescing soldiers were taken into the hearts of the people of Walton. The cycle shop designed and lent patients rickshaws. There were also river trips to Windsor, and local rowers would take the soldiers boating. There are even accounts of soldiers performing a farewell "gang show," dressing up in nurses' uniforms and singing and dancing to say thank you. After leaving, some returned home, while others headed bravely back to battle.

I jolt out of my daze. "So I guess when I'm out there it would be fun to see if there's any link anywhere with Walton. I've also been lucky to meet a handful of New Zealanders while I've been out on the road this summer who've given me incredible tips on what to do and see "under the radar." You know me, I don't want to look too much at the normal "lay of the land" through the likes of Google Earth, or where will the surprise be? That'll come soon enough."

We both remain silent for a while. Lulu finally smiles upwards. "All those stars and planets up in the Milky Way—it's so beautiful. Remember, when you're there, you'll be staring up at the Southern Cross while I'll be staring up at the North Star.

2017. Walton-on-Thames. December.

Just another month before I jump on that plane to Christchurch to pick up the motorcycle and start the journey. I'll be riding the new Bonneville T100 900cc, although deep down I've already started having a few reservations on its size and weight for such potentially varied terrain. But we'll see.

It's at this same time that I also start communicating with Sean, the sub-editor of the New Zealand *Bike Rider Magazine*, of whom I'd asked advice for on anything to enhance my trip.

The light-hearted notes that jump back are quirky and just up my street and he's certainly never short of a word or two . . .

3 December. Hey Zoë—I'm Sean & the Big Cheese has passed your details to me so, I guess I'm your new word wrangler as far as the magazine is concerned. Sounds like you've got an interesting trip planned. First trip to the Antipodes? Let me know your time frame and where you wanna go. I'll try & help. Right, so now a quick crash course in Maori which is technically pronounced Mow-ri. Kia Ora is hello (key orah) is our casual gidday in Kiwi and can be used to say thank you but it's not so common so it's usually a greeting. Haere Mai (Hi reh My) is welcome which is semi-formal and Here Ra (Hi Reh Rah) is goodbye and safe travels.

Oh yea remember, when riding here, we ride on the left. In the South Island especially, stay well clear of the centre line. Too many campervans rented by tourists who tend to cross over.

8 Dec. Hi Sean. That's brilliant news. Yes it's the very first time in the Antipodes for me. I arrive in NZ on the 5 January with a month on the North Island, then biking back down for a month in the South Island including the Burt Munro Challenge weekend so hopefully we'll have a chance to meet. Where you based?

10 Dec. Hey Zoë—sounds cool. I currently live in Hamilton which is on the upper mid part of the North Island. There are a couple of things you need to know to make things a little easier. First thing is your "roads less travelled" theme is going to be a little bit of a challenge because most of NZ has already been toured! You don't get to go far in this little country before you hit roads that are somewhat more than travelled! Our State Highway network is pretty comprehensive. But my previous life of a motorcycle rental agent meant I always had to find alternative routes to the main highways so maybe I can help! I'm most familiar with the North Island as are most North Islanders because for us, getting to the South Island is actually quite expensive. Also, besides everything else I'm sure you've got planned, a "must do" route for you in the South Island is the "Starlight Highway". As a Kiwi, I would be doing this in a heartbeat, because even us locals don't get to see the night sky like this!

14 Dec. Hey Zoë—this is what happens when sub-editors get bored so hope you liked the attached suggestions for your first few days. You can ignore them but do so at your peril as this is the sort of thing I'd be looking to do if it was me in your boots. I guess you can now call me your "Ghost Rider" buddy who'll be following you out on the road providing all those dazzling tips! Just shout if you have any specific interests that you want a kiwi take on. I can definitely steer you in the right direction. Planes, trains and automobiles? Viticulture? Llamas? Chocolate? . . . and I assume you'll want to see some hobbits! See ya! GR

I smile and stare back at my possessions, knowing only too soon I'll be unpacking them on the other side of the world.

PART ONE

THE NORTH ISLAND

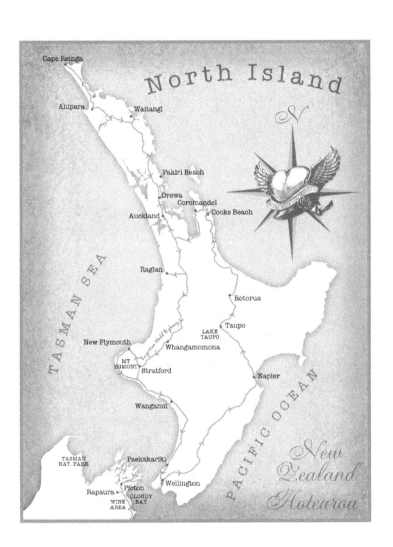

1

EXPECT THE UNEXPECTED

FIRST NIGHT IN PRISON—CYCLONE NUMBER 1 DELAYS—EARTHQUAKES

The departures lounge at London Heathrow, already full to capacity, is organized chaos as my eyes quickly scan over the room for a spare seat among the hundreds of pink dressed Aussies, screaming kids, and pajama clad Brits for this mega three day flight via Melbourne. I spot one and dash in and out of hand luggage, grab it, and sit down panting. I've bizarrely planted myself next to the only person who looks, with my current naivety on the subject, to be a Maori from New Zealand or maybe the Pacific Islands. He's heavily inked with a beautiful tattooed fish swimming down his muscular arm.

Nodding his head to the rhythm of music from his massive ear hugging headphones, he smiles, noticing the helmet next to me, and watches me casually flick through my *Lonely Planet* guide. He silently taps his fingers to the music, like he's thinking, then rips a page from his magazine and quickly scribbles something onto it.

Sliding his headphones off, he passes the piece of paper to me "Gidday mate, how ya doing? Now if you really wanna get to see our place for real you gotta check these classics out. Tu meke & ride safe."

Ten strange things are listed. I smile with curiosity. Sheep—Pohutukawa—Kiwi—Number 8—Paua—Jandals—Silver Fern—Swanndri—Taranaki Gate—The Bach. Most I'd never heard of, but I am teased to maybe track them down along the way and find out more. I'm just about to ask a few questions when we're called to the plane and my mate's jumped up and rushed to the gate.

I race to jump in and slam the taxi door shut from the pouring, cold rain at Christchurch airport. It's pitch dark and still very early.

"Morning; where you going?"

"Just take me to the Jailhouse."

He smiles and nods. On the floor my foot kicks a crumpled newspaper. I lean down to pick it up. It's yesterday's, 4th January, *New Zealand Herald*. I sit back in shock as we drive through dark residential streets. The front page headlines shout out:

> *Wild weather: as the year's first storm hits, woman dies after tree fall as wind, tides, rain smash North Island—Kaiaua is cut off by rising flood-waters and residents in low-lying parts told to evacuate—Major roads across the North Island have been closed by flooding and toppled trees—King tides, gales and driving rain continue to cause widespread damage—Thousands without power as power lines topple in hurricane with strong winds blasting the island—Camper and trampers are warned to be aware of the deteriorating conditions.*

I gulp. I'm supposed to be starting the first leg of my journey and heading out in that direction tomorrow! The cab stops in front of the Jailhouse Hostel, a genuine old prison, and I dart in to check into my own authentic cell, complete with a small barred window at the top. I'm exhausted, having not slept since Wednesday morning and its now Friday.

A shadowy silhouette appears from the lower bunk and without a word leaves, just as I'm climbing up into the bed above to get some desperate shut eye—but no luck. I toss and turn. In just a few hours I'm going to be picked up by the guys from the rental company to collect the bike. I'm telling myself I'll need to be mentally and physically strong to then ride it and find my own way back here in the storm.

A jeep's horn blasts at 9 AM exactly, and dressed in my motorcycle gear, I jump in next to Carole, who runs South Pacific Motorcycle Tours where I'd sourced the Bonneville. The windscreen wipers are working overtime.

"Hey, Zoë, welcome to New Zealand. It's only a forty minute drive to Swannanoa, where our outfit is. The bike's been prepped, and we'll just talk you through about maybe what's different about biking in New Zealand and things to look out for."

I smile awkwardly. "Great to see you too, Carole. But this weather isn't good, and I'm supposed to be leaving tomorrow to head northwards up along the coast."

She nods and replies casually, "Well, maybe you should just stick around here a bit and wait it out."

I also nod, but for practicality's sake; I don't agree, as the trip's plan would have to be modified. I've a tight, heavy schedule, and in this busy holiday season to ensure I could cross over onto the North Island the day after next, I was forced to book my ferry crossing months ago. Optimistically, I feel convinced a lot could change in twenty-four hours.

Entering the driveway to the garage block, a spanking new black 900cc Triumph Bonneville, with two robust touring hard panniers, is standing ready and to attention. But the news is not good.

Carole's husband walks up to me and shakes my hand firmly. "How you doing? What a trip you've got planned! Normally we'd have given you the keys now, and you could have just ridden off, but we're seriously worried about the current storms, the flooded roads, and your safety. I'd even go to say it's definitely not recommended for you to ride back into Christchurch on your own to the hostel! All this weather is unprecedented. Listen, we'll drive you back, we'll keep tabs on the weather reports, and then if it clears a bit, we'll deliver the bike to you later on in the day. That'll also give you a chance to see a bit of Christchurch, even if it is under an umbrella!"

I sigh even more nervously and silently nod my head in agreement.

He smiles back. "But we'll make it happen and for now can help you get prepped. So where are you planning to stop off first?"

"Well, the plan's to get up onto the North Island as soon as possible, where I'll be spending the first month. The first day I just want to get used to the bike and, ideally, have an easy run from here to reach Kaikoura. Then the next day it's up to Picton to catch the boat."

He carefully considers this with a surprising answer, "Well, to know your possible routes and which ones are open you'll need to call the government's helpline just before you're leaving Christchurch. But I can tell you that there are basically two options; the Inland Road, Route 70, which is open seven days a week but a lot longer and mountainous, or State Highway 1, which became engulfed by the 7.8 magnitude earthquake that hit Kaikoura in November 2016. It totally devastated and closed this part of our country's backbone road. But lucky for you, it opened just a few weeks ago in December but will still be under construction throughout 2018. So expect some unsealed surfaces, quite a lot of lane closures with Stop and Go controls, and speed restrictions. There are two sections closed every night for safety, so make sure you travel outside those times."

I gulp, not for the first time, while he continues, "But SH1 opening hours can be affected by weather or seismic activity, so they only put the news out on the same day to tell you if the road is open. But whatever happens, expect delays! There're two building-sections for cliff face stabilisation and road re-building before you even get to Kaikoura and then a new overbridge build with road realignment and new seawall build a bit further on before you get to Picton. You'll need to allow yourself at least an hour through both sections."

I'm then told a few things about what's different about riding in New Zealand, like giving way at intersections, overtaking, riding speeds, keeping left, and to be aware of the numerous single lane bridges and always, to keep well on my side of the road!

We shake hands, with my fingers crossed on the other that I'll be hooked up with the bike later, and then I'm given a lift back to windblown Christchurch. Just an hour later, with a small city map held in my gloved hands, I'm trudging the cold, wet streets under the raining, grey, cloud covered skies looking at the devastation that wreaked havoc in 2011, resulting in the deaths of 185 people. There are still enormous areas that are totally empty where the rubble and debris have been removed. A carpark in Hereford Street strangely still has a solitary graffiti painted concrete staircase that must have been once part of a massive building.

The severely damaged neo-gothic Cathedral was also hit and cordoned off behind fencing in the middle of a busy ring road, and without its collapsed tower, forlornly stands covered in weeds. Time's limited, and the weather isn't making this too enjoyable, so after popping into a bar for a strong mojito and tortillas, I head to the one place I didn't want to miss. On Latimer Square is the Paper Cathedral. It's the only one in the world made of cardboard. A Japanese "emergency architect," Shigeru Ban, who'd built something similar after the Kobe earthquake, offered to design a replacement cathedral. Remarkably, just two years later it was completed on this main thoroughfare of Christchurch. Walking through this airy, light, and uplifting building I'm amazed in seeing the waves of cardboard tubes combined with local wood and steel making it earthquake safe and quite an architectural feat! But it's cold, and I need a hot drink. I smile as I walk into the aptly named "Hell" coffee shop.

Six hours later, my heart palpitates both in trepidation and excitement as I watch the bike being taken off the van and the keys are handed to me. Kim smiles, "Now remember, we're here if you need anything and, most importantly, just keep a daily check up on the weather. It can change quickly here. See you in a couple of months." And with that they're gone.

Tonight I'm kept awake by strong winds banging the prison windows with the new Mrs. Cellmate snoring heavily in the bunkbed below. I don't know which is worse!

2

RACING THE STORM

GHOST RIDER—DESTROYED ROADS
CRAYFISH—CHRISTMAS TREES

I turn the ignition and a deep roar explodes from the black beast's belly. I would be lying to say I'm not a little nervous and uncomfortable, which is valid for a number of reasons.

Firstly, I'm already questioning the selection of the motorcycle! The Bonneville with all its luggage is a heavy bike, and from experience, I know I wouldn't be able to lift it up if it fell or crashed onto me. Full of petrol it weighs 230 kilos, and that's without at least another extra 15 kilos of my stuff. That's more than three times my own weight! For a number of reasons and including that one, I'd sold my own beloved T100 café racer just a few months back and exchanged it for the lighter, lower, and more agile Honda Rebel bobber, which was currently being customized back in London.

Secondly, I have no idea what the quality of the roads is going to be like, what I'll encounter, and if needing to urgently manoeuvre "The Beast" at any time in awkward terrain I'll need to do that balancing on my tippy toes! Will I be strong enough? But one thing I already have a gut feel about is that these roads aren't going to be the long, straight rounds I've encountered across North America. Then there's this unpredictable and surprising weather. It's making news around the world. Only late last night, my friend, Brent in Milwaukee, had messaged me stating New Zealand, with its severe storms, was currently even being featured in their news and to be careful.

Anyway, fortunately on this early Saturday morning and the big day of departure, the rain has stopped pelting down, but the wind remains strong and unpredictable. The aim for the next couple of days is to safely get through the earthquake zones to the northern tip of the South Island and catch the ferry in Picton, which represents about 400 kilometres in distance. I tighten my luggage straps over and around my bag on my seat behind me and, with no sat-nav, simply look down at the map inserted in my tank bag. From my jacket I pull out the helpful notes that Sean, my Ghost Rider buddy, had provided. My goal today is to reach Kaikoura, about halfway up the Pacific east coast.

The transport helpline confirms that Highway 1 is open today, which makes me happy. So that's the route I'll take. I push my left foot down on the gear selector, then kick it up twice, and leave Lincoln Road at a slow, steady pace, feeling the initial power of the bike underneath me and the equally powerful gusts of wind pushing me around.

Just past Christchurch airport my prayers are answered, and the sky turns to a miraculous cloudy washed-out blue. It's still blustery, but this must surely be a good omen that the weather's turning. The city disappears from my rear-view mirror, and very quickly the rolling countryside takes its place. The road is quiet, smooth, and flat as I cross the massive Waimakariri (y mach ah ree ree) River that's flowed from the Southern Alps to join the sea and then ride through the little settlement of Kaiapoi, famous for its merino wool products. Every now and again, polite signs warn me not to exceed 100 km/h through farmlands with their verdant green pastures full of sheep, deer, horses, and the white-faced Hereford cattle.

It's at Waipara, with mountains starting to rear their heads out in the distance, that State Highway 1 now splits, with the option to head inland and get closer to them along SH7. But since receiving the news that the road was fully open along the coast, I've already decided to carry on. The place already feels wild. This largely inland part of the route is beautiful, and I take it steadily until I reach the pretty but quiet township of Cheviot in the district of Canterbury. I've almost forgotten the taste of that bacon toastie that I'd devoured at Burger King before leaving Christchurch, so it's time for a brew at the rustic Paddock Café. I park the bike directly outside, without a single other vehicle in the vicinity. They must have all parked out at the back, because inside this place is heaving!

Stoked up, I continue passing a number of smaller settlements and am dumbfounded in seeing so few cars out on the roads, even though it's high season. May this continue! Very shortly and for the first time I start to climb up, round, and over twisting, winding hills. Nothing massive, just a teaser, but I am starting to see just a small change in the previously very flat landscape. It's then the Pacific Ocean appears directly next to me with its waves pounding relentlessly up against the rocky coastline. And just a few hundred metres ahead, a car has stopped at a red light. We've arrived at Goose Bay, one of the areas worst hit by the earthquake. Orange cone bollards are stuck in the middle of the road as another car approaches from the opposite direction and slowly passes us.

This gives me time to pull up my visor to look around and witness the mass devastation. Dozens and dozens of large metal containers stand on either side of the road, and the huge cliff face in front looks like it's only being supported from crashing down by massive metal web netting and concrete boulders. The tunnel running into the cliff is barricaded and closed off. There's now only one narrow gritty lane hugging the steep, rocky sea edge. Finally, the light turns green, we all start up our engines, and slowly but cautiously follow each other for about a mile along this precarious and fragile part of the coast. Besides a few large stones that I successfully avoid, I get to the other side unscathed.

The road really is now cuddling the coast, and it feels exciting. Before long, under ever more ominous stormy skies, the coastline flattens out revealing strange black sandy beaches bordered by tall conifers with layer upon layer of majestic mountains standing out in the background and welcoming me to Kaikoura.

Torquay Street is just a block back from the beach as I park the bike in the courtyard of the Albatross Inn, formerly the old post office, hoping in no time at all that I'll be chowing down on the famous crayfish. A friendly guy shows me to my dorm, where

I'm greeted by three smiling girls who are backpacking across the country from Canton, Hong Kong, and Korea.

I dump my luggage and walk back to reception. "Hey Geoff, Where can I find some decent crayfish to eat?"

He smiles, "Well there is a secret spot where the crayfish man and his van normally park up further along the peninsula on Tyffe Quay. But I'm not sure he'll be there. Kaikoura's had it really hard since the quake. We're really dependent on the tourism dollar, and when you get cut off as we did, well, it kinda really sucks. The community here was cut off for one year, one month, and one day! The Government's fast tracked road repairs, and the whole country was amazingly behind our survival. Apparently, the quake was big enough that the seafloor has actually now come up to become part of the mainland!"

With a hungry stomach to keep me company, I take an amble along the coastline towards the peninsula. It's a very long walk, and when I finally arrive at a small car park on the side of the road, I'm annoyed to see there's no damn crayfish, but only a sign apologizing that crayfish man won't be here for the next two Saturdays. Besides sheep shearing demos in the farm across the road, there's not much else here, so I turn back. Passing the old Pier Hotel, overlooking Ingles Bay and the dramatic Kaikoura Ranges, without hesitation I pop in for a well-deserved beer and mussel chowder.

Then it's a little wander into the town to visit the museum to learn more about New Zealand's largest and longest earthquake that shattered this community on 14 November 2016. Along the way is a rustic, wood panelled beach house with borders bursting full of massive beautiful purple and white flowers. An old man is working in the garden. He looks up. I smile and wave, and being a bit of a gardener myself, congratulate him, "Wow. Those are beautiful flowers you've got growing there."

Surprisingly, he huffs in contempt and says, "Funny you say that, but these Agapanthus, a sort of lily from South Africa, grow everywhere here. They're like our weeds! Can't get rid of 'em!"

Along the sea walk into a park I wander under an archway of massive whale rib bones, which proudly shows this was an important whaling station in the 1840s. Waiopuka Beach is known as a whale cemetery, and occasionally, stormy seas uncover bones that have lain under the sand for more than a century—a silent testimony of an industry and changing values that we'll never see again.

But what I am beginning to notice here in New Zealand are the strongly intertwined lives, beliefs, stories, and mythology of the brave explorers who first travelled from the distant South Pacific Islands, and then a lot later, the European voyagers and settlers. In the park I see a decorated panel that tells the story of the naming of Kaikouri—"the name Kai (food) Koura (crayfish) has its origin in the story of Tamatea-Pokai-Whenua, who in 1450, stopped off at the peninsula to feed on crayfish on his way south to search for three of his wives who had fled. Bent on recapturing the wayward women, he pursued them down the East Coast, through Foveaux Strait, then north up the West Coast. All to no avail, as he found one had turned to greenstone at Milford. As he paused to 'tangi' (weep) over her, some of the tears fell on the stone which has carried the marks ever since. He came upon his other wives at Ahaura River where they, together with their canoe, had also been turned to greenstone. The names of Tamatea's three wives are now used to specify the three principal kinds of greenstone: Tangiwai, Kahurangi, and Kawakawa."

Later that night, I can't resist a generous helping of local blue cod with a scoop of chips wrapped in paper to eat on the black beach while watching the sunset.

My eyelids flutter open, and I feel like it's Groundhog Day. I'm sat on my bike with the same huge mountains on one side and pounding ocean on the other waiting to navigate yet another stretch of identical rubbly earthquake-hit road, this time at Irongate, just outside Kaikoura. I pull up my visor and curiously shout over to one of the workmen, "When's it gonna get finished?"

Turning the sign to "GO," he shouts back, "God knows!" I and a couple of cars are then led by a truck and its flashing lights round the curving coastal road out of danger.

But before all this, the day had started later than planned. Amusingly, I'd been misled to believe it was raining outside, so stayed nestled in bed, only to find it was just the noisy sound of the AC! Opening the shutters, the storm had been swept away, leaving sunshine and bright blue skies. I'd also filled up for the first time, paying $2.2 a litre, and this was continuing to make me realize that this wasn't a very cheap place to buy stuff.

The landscape has now opened up, and green rounded hills are rolling into each other with evermore white, fluffy sheep dotted around them. Suddenly, I look around startled and see a hazy ghostly-looking motorcycle race towards me. Ghost Rider has appeared out of nowhere, and riding nonchalantly with his feet up on the tank shouts out, "Up to Picton is largely coastal road, so take it easy, you might encounter the odd sea lion sunbathing in the centreline, nahh, I'm kidding, they've got their tanning salons on the beach. But I do counsel caution, as the road is pretty new."

True to his word, my jaw opens gobsmacked. This is probably one of the most amazing places I've seen so far. It's difficult to put into words. The roads splits the fields and mountains on one side with the sea on the other. Everything, all in one place. I'm getting a feel for the bike, and it's now lapping up the miles.

He continues, "This entire region has 'alternative' accommodation, including glamping and freedom camping, which attracts so many tourists to New Zealand. But eventually you'll get fed up with our version of the Cornwall coast and begin to wonder when this damn Picton place is gonna show up. Soon after Clarence, you'll come to the coast border of Canterbury and Marlborough. No border guards, so your passport can stay in your pack. It might be a little warmer too as you pass though."

Technically in Wharanui (Far ahnoo ey), the cute St. Oswalds church peeps out from between fields on the outskirts of Ward. Once again, my Ghost Rider apparition appears from nowhere and riding up alongside me pulls up his visor, "Your next POI is here in Ward. Back in 1905 the prime minister of New Zealand, Dick Seddon, named this place in honour of his mate, Joseph Ward. The story goes that the name "Ward" has never been officially registered, which is good news, because the locals want the name changed to Flaxbourne for the nearby river. 'King Dick' is historically recognized as the longest serving PM here, with over thirteen years in office. He was responsible for establishing our state supported welfare system and was particularly admired by the Maori people. He was a busy boy, serving as Minister of Native Affairs, as well as Public Works, Mines, and Defense."

With that, he puts his visor and foot down, accelerates at supersonic speed and disappears out into the distance, while I continue kissing the coast with a fast run along Highway 1 to Seddon.

Once again looking in my mirror, Ghost Rider appears from behind, racing at breakneck speed and only slowing down to narrowly miss me, "This is one of the stop points for our Coastal

Pacific tourist train. Rail travel is expensive for New Zealanders, though most of us would love to do something like the Coastal Pacific or the Transalpine trip.

"Back in the day, during the 70s, going from Auckland to Wellington by train was actually very doable. You'd take the Silver Fern, which offered sleeper cars. It was no longer than a National Airways Corporation flight, but cheaper, and because of the car situation at the time—yes at the time we had car-less days, on account of being so far away from the rest of the world's fuel! The trains were a lifeblood for all manner of travellers. As cars became more common and the global village got smaller, the trains fell into disuse. But they've started to make a comeback on account of their novelty. Wellington, in the north, still has a very strong commuter train system, probably the strongest in the country. Christchurch is too seismically unstable now, and Auckland has got all those commuter trains. Right, I gotta fly. Your next stop is Blenheim, home of hops, tobacco, and wine. See you there!" And he disappears.

Approaching Blenheim, I stop on the side of the road. A big decision needs to be made: to simply continue just twenty minutes north on this fairly hassle-free straight road all the way to Picton or to make a detour up along the demanding Marlborough Sounds coastal road. I look at the map for answers but instead see a ghostly image in front of me.

Ghost Rider is already parked up, casually eating fish and chips from paper, "Believe me, or believe your gut instinct, and take the alternative little trip on SH6. You'll go through the sleepy-ish Blenheim, home to a bunch of viticulturists, with Wither Hills Wines and Cloudy Bay being the big names of note. It was once considered the gateway to the South, but Picton's now claimed that title. Head west towards Woodbourne. If you have time, ride through the vineyards to Omaka Aerodrome, which is home to a really good display of aircraft and dioramas and what I'd call a highlight of the area. New Zealand, of course, has an obsession with flight. Richard Pearse, the pioneer who flew about three days before the Wright brothers, but nobody knew, and of course, we have our own aviatrix, Jean Batten. Kiwis were also there in World War I and World War II. I think 'Cobber' Kain, fighter and flying ace extraordinaire, was one of ours, and there was Sir Keith Park, along with a bunch of guys from RAF Bomber Command. So as you can imagine, we have a lot of air-dedicated museums with classic aircraft from all eras. At Omaka, you'll likely get a great snap or two with a classic aircraft of some description much more easily than anywhere else, if that spins your wheels.

"The other reason for sending you this way is to give you a shot at Queen Charlotte Drive. There are a handful of 'must rides' in New Zealand, and this is one of them! That'll take you into Picton from the north for your overnight stay before crossing the Cook Strait."

And with that and in a blink of an eye he's disappeared into the ether. I smile and now confidently head west into the rich land of vineyards, pop into the Omaka Aviation Heritage Centre with planes dotted everywhere for a cheeky snap or two with the bike, and continue northwards through Havelock, famous for its green-lipped mussels. And it's here I start riding the steep, windy majestic roads clinging onto and along the Marlborough Sounds. The far-reaching landscapes with islands dotted out to sea are mesmerizing with wonderful viewpoints to pull over onto.

There's a Maori legend that tells of a great waka (canoe), belonging to Maori gods of ancient heaven, that formed this place, emerging from the mists of distant time. So long was the journey and so far were the paddlers from their source of power, that they were trapped on earth. A storm capsized the vessel. Its beautiful, intricately carved prow shattered and partially sank to form the waterways and islands known today as Marlborough Sounds.

But it's also here, and for the first time, that I start to experience the feeling of those massive campervans following closely and impatiently behind me, and it doesn't feel good. I turn into the final viewpoint to also get away from them. Picton's ferry terminal and yacht and gin palace-filled marina are far below, with the towering semi-tropical green hills hugging and licking the shoreline.

The bike hums through the streets of this small compact town, still lined with bauble-decorated Christmas trees, and comes to a stop at the old hospital, now simply just a Spanish-themed backpackers hostel. Ominously, it's here I have my first anxious suspicions of the bike's weight and manoeuvrability on less than solid ground. The only access is up a massively steep, shifting gravelly driveway. I'm palpitating with fear. It's too much for me. I park it out on the road together with the stress.

My first job is to go find some of these green-lipped mussels, a cheeky glass of local wine, and then kick back and relax under one of the palm trees, looking out to the boats bobbing up and down on the calm Marlborough Sounds.

3

Island Hopping

Tunnel Run—Queen's Corgis
Art Deco—Nein nein nein!

It's dead quiet and for me one of the best times of the day before everyone's woken up. And here on Main Street, as I leisurely drink my first coffee, I curiously look around and take in the place. Across the road there's a motel that looks more like the convenient "one-hour" rooms I'd seen in South East Asia, the "Roll In and Pig Out" Pub, the Med Lab for "Blood Tests," and the "Indulge" ice-cream parlour. The Christmas trees run down to the beach, mingling with the swaying palm trees, and with the bright blue sky it's strange to see them in this hot tropical place.

But all of a sudden, the tranquillity has gone. The tables fill up with OAPs in their regulatory khaki shorts, smart chequered short-sleeved shirts, and socks pulled high over pristine white trainers. That signals it's time for me to leave, and I jump on the loaded bike to head towards the port, but not before filling the tank with seven litres of fuel and lightening my wallet by fifteen dollars.

I ride over to the waiting point and see just two other bikes. In just under an hour, the boat's leaving at 11:15AM, and it's already hot, with three people dressed in full biker gear sitting patiently in the shade of the "biker's hut." Like with all bikers, conversation flows easily. They're all heading home. Richard, the solo traveller, is from Normanby, near New Plymouth, and Leon and Debra are two friendly South Africans who live just outside Auckland in Beach Haven where, coincidentally, I'll be staying! Before long, all three bikes are signalled to ride up into this massive boat before the giant trucks with their containers join us. Following Leon, I carefully ride up the knobbly floor, enter the ship's stomach, and park next to him. Trying to look like an expert, I take out my straps to secure the bike. It had been recommended to take a set, as the ones belonging to the boats would often be old and dirty, if not hard to find. Richard sees me dithering and kindly helps to tie the bike down, which makes me feel better that there's at least one person who knows what they're doing!

The boat leaves punctually and begins an incredible three-and a-half-hour crossing through the mountainous and forest lined Marlborough Sounds and out across the Cook Strait. I find my way out onto the upper deck feeling the wonderful warm breeze, and gaze out to the turquoise waters.

Leaning over the rails looking out to sea is Michael, one of the ship's hands. Attired in a set of zip-up orange and blue overalls, a walkie-talkie around his neck, and a cup of coffee in his big strong hands, with his silver white hair and thick moustache he looks around and smiles. "It's good and sunny this morning, eh?" I nod. "You may even see some dolphins as we get out. Take it easy." And he walks away.

Through the spectacular Hamilton Straits it's not long before the views of Wellington appear, and all four of us excitedly go running down to untie our bikes. Debra stuffs a piece of paper into my hand and rushes to help Leon. I unfold it: "So here's my number for when you're in Beach Haven. I'm happy to show you all the gorgeous parts of it, and all the bush walk and beaches. I love it here. This is our address . . . Chat soon and stay safe X". I slide the note carefully into my jacket pocket.

The mouth of the boat opens up, spits us out, and we ride off entering busy built-up areas and past Custom House Quay. My mission is to head towards Wellington's downtown district and up to Mount Victoria, where I'll be staying overnight. At the next intersection Leon waves goodbye then crazily points his hand in the direction I need to head towards. Checking the map on the tank, I continue past Te Papa Tongarewa, the Museum of New Zealand, before climbing up hilly residential roads to the very top at Pirie Street. This is definitely the place, but I just can't find the number, so naively and slowly, thinking it's on the other side, ride through the dark, rubbly one-lane Mount Victoria Tunnel! I stop on the other side, knowing this can't be right. And that's confirmed as a bus rushes past me hammering its horn at me. It's then I realize this tunnel road is just for buses and I've no idea how the hell to get back onto the other side through the other side of the city. There's nothing else I can do but call Jane, my hostess.

Luckily, she answers her phone. "I'm really sorry, and it's a good start to only having just arrived here in Wellington, but I'm on the other side of Pirie Street through the tunnel. Can you help me?"

"Wow!" she shouts in a high pitch voice, "That's wrong! We're just next to the tunnel on the left. You went straight past us. Listen. You'll never find us now. Hang on, and I'll drive round to collect you. Give me fifteen minutes."

And true to her word, just a bit later, a little car arrives and leads me through Wellington, back up to her beautiful Victorian house standing at the top of the hill. That afternoon it's simply a wonderful walk exploring this quaint little city. Just five minutes away, I enter Mt. Victoria Park with its forests and landscapes that provided many locations for the Outer Shire in *The Hobbit* and walk down a track where the hobbits had to escape Nazgul with the worms and spiders escaping from the ground in revulsion of his evilness. Zig-zagging down the shaded woodland footpaths and then out onto the little residential streets, I come down to the shoreline and Oriental Bay Beach, past the marina, and pop into the museum to see beautiful Maori art. It's also here where John Britten's world-record breaking bike is displayed, the Britten V1000, which had been "built like a torpedo atop a knife blade." Then it's past rows of container shops, comical sharks painted on a wall, and then a stop at Wellington Writers Walk, where I need to take a second look. Climbing up steep steps is a line of guys jumping off it recklessly into the murky waters below. A couple of beer bellied Maoris with long shorts and long hair tied back look down, curiously waiting for their go to jump or belly flop in. It's certainly drawing a crowd.

Walking back exhausted later that evening from seeing so much of this eclectic place, I finally queue up at the renowned Mt. Vic Chippery for their famous tempura battered Tarakkihi and hand-cut Agria chips. Biting into the moist delicious fish, this was certainly worth the wait.

The next morning, Jane, an acclaimed local writer with books crammed everywhere around the house, provides a hearty breakfast for me and two Americans from San Francisco. Without thinking too much about it, but due to their curiosity on what I've been up to, I tell them about the previous breakfast I'd had in Picton and seeing all those people wearing those awful big shorts. Before I know it, I've looked down and embarrassingly realize they're dressed exactly the same! But there are no bad feelings, and we all laugh it off with an extra dollop of scrambled egg!

So with that I wave the lovely little capital city of Wellington goodbye and jump onto State Highway 2, almost immediately hitting the massive mountainous Remutaka Range running parallel to the east coast. This was something I was certainly not expecting so early on in the trip.

I can only describe the slow progress on the long winding roads as tortuous. I'm nervous in keeping the bike accelerated enough to climb but slow enough to control with its heavy luggage round these twisty bends. But the views across these tropical tree lined slopes are spectacular. There are no real stop-off points, and so I just keep my hands tightly on the handlebars and breathe deeply, accepting that any cars behind me will just have to overtake me!

But I start smiling at Mount Bruce when I see my first kiwi bird, even if it is only a road sign. I'll make damn sure not to run one over, which I'm guessing is highly unlikely.

Around one of the last tight bends, my Ghost Rider reassuringly appears alongside me. "Hey, you're doing great. Remember there are alternative routes heading east on your way to Napier when you reach Masterton. But maybe you should head for Ekatahuna, famous for being not a town but a state of mind! From Hastings it's just a short run to Napier on State Highway 2, which is mostly coastal. See ya later alligator!" And he vanishes into thin air.

So at Masterton, still not fully committed on which route to take, I fill up and hand some notes to an old lady at the garage. "Well, you see, if it was me, I'd avoid the 52. It'll take you longer, and I've heard there's a diversion along part of it and so it's not all paved."

Great, the decision's been made for me. So I continue up to Ekatahuna. It feels like a lost place in the middle of nowhere. I'm dying for a wee, so I park up and, instead of finding the usual tree or bush, walk along the street to the strangest set of public toilets. One of the queen's royal guards with his bearskin hat on and holding her corgis is painted on the wall. And inside them a local radio station is blasting music out in the toilets that makes me tap my foot while

I'm seated on the throne. I walk back to the bike and sit down at "Addiction Café" for a couple of naughty homemade cakes and a strong brew.

Waiting for my mug of coffee, a guy in a navy blue uniform with the obligatory sunglasses on his head is seated at the table next to me scoffing, "The Big Brekkie." He looks up and nods, "Kia ora."

I smile. He's a Maori, and I nod in return, "Hi. So do you work around here?"

He quickly chews and swallows his food, stretching out his arm to shake my hand hearing my accent. "Hi. I'm Reg. Well, not exactly. I started this new sales job just three weeks ago selling lorries. It means I've got to travel quite a bit."

"This place is pretty interesting. It looks like they're sprucing it up."

"Yea, you could say that. They call it a lost place. Back in time it used to have a railway so was a central meeting point for the farmers. It had all the shops, including a butchers. But with the start of the highways and cars it started to die, as no one needed to stop here."

This is reminding me of the stories I'd heard about Route 66 in America.

He continues, "But it's now coming back to life, and people like to see this old place. This café is helping to get people to stop along the way."

I agree with a smile. He wipes his mouth clean and leaves, keeping the door open for another guy coming in with paint-stained trousers. Without a word, this guy smiles to the hipster behind the bar, who hands him a guitar that he spontaneously starts to play and sing along to. Crazy or what?

Swinging my leg over the seat to leave, an older guy comes out of the woodwork in this lost, empty place and wanders up to me. He looks the bike over. "Well I never! I used to ride old Triumphs. But I've got something to say to you, young lady. Be careful and let 'em pass! They're all now fast, fast, fast, and all want to get from A to B without seeing the journey's route. Keep it in mind." I nod in respect, and he wanders off, looking back just one last time.

By eleven, it's drizzling, and I'm already getting into the habit of pulling those waterproofs on, just in case. Approaching Woodville, I have to stop. There, across the fields and stretching over the distant mountains, I see my first dramatic long thin white cloud, for which this country is synonymous. Its Polynesian discoverers called the place "Aotearoa"—the land of the long white cloud. Such a cloud, riding on the prevailing westerlies above New Zealand's spine, told those first explorers of the Pacific that land lay in the distant south-western corner of the world's largest ocean—two large fertile lands, hospitable to man, and one of the last of the world's major inhabitable areas to feel the tread of human feet.

But the heavy black clouds above it are ominous, and I now just want to reach Napier. I follow a milk tanker for a while before it turns off and then Dannevirke, another small settlement, appears. There's, again, not much happening, except for yet another bizarre spectacle. There, on the pavement outside the doors of the bank, is a little girl, no more than eight or ten years old, belting out a song into a microphone with not one spectator. Why? For what? I don't know. Continuing on across the green pastures and prairies, the riding is becoming more intense. Rushing, impatient traffic appears and narrowly overtakes. Massive double trailer sheep trucks race past in the opposite direction, knocking me sideways with the strength of the wind passing between us. Concentrate. Keep going. And I need some water. I'm starting to see these roads need to be respected.

Another hundred kilometres and I pass Hastings, which Ghost Rider had told me was close to Te Mata Peak, or Tomato Peak. This would offer me a non-paying tourist thing, to see the lay of the land and maybe watch some people up there who like throwing themselves off high places under canvas. But the short coastal "sprint" starts, and I just keep going until I'm cruising through palm fringed avenues with a long white beach on one side and art deco buildings on the other, including a miniature size replica of what I think looks like the famous Hotel Negresco in Cannes. I head to Lucy Road, where I'll be staying, but it's a massive steep hill with only traffic heading downwards. It's not difficult to see it's a one way road, and I've no idea in hell on how to get onto it from the the bottom. I park the bike and take a recce walk up it to, literally, see the lay of the land. The cottage I need to get to is on a steep incline, with an even steeper gradient track leading down to it. This is a nightmare for me and the heavy bike. I'm stressed and don't feel good with this and the difficult mountainous journey I've just ridden. The explanation on Airbnb was wrong when it said it had easy access for bikes. The road's so steep I almost come back down on my bum and once there I simply decide to leave the bike where it is and just pull out some essentials for this one night stop over!

The bell rings and a girl rushes to open the door and just as quickly shows me a little room. She apologizes but will soon be out all evening and to make myself at home. I walk out to a spectacular multi-terraced garden looking out to sea and take a long deep breath. I slap cold water onto my face and decide to walk back into Napier to grab some lunch and take a look around. This is a really pretty seaside town, as I pass the national Aquarium and rows of seafront restaurants, and exudes a completely different atmosphere from the previous places I've already been to. I grab a table outside the iconic Emporium Eatery on Tennyson Street and chow down on fresh calamari. But what I've really come here for is to witness the architecture. A natural disaster resulted in Napier becoming one of the purest Art Deco cities in the world. In 1931, a massive earthquake rocked Hawke's Bay for more than three minutes, killing nearly 260 and destroying the commercial centre of Napier.

Rebuilding began almost immediately, and new buildings reflected the architectural styles of the times—stripped classical, Spanish mission, and art deco. The local architect Louis Hay, a fan of the great Frank Lloyd Wright, had been given his chance to shine. Maori motifs were used to give the place a unique New Zealand character, which I see on the bank on the corner of Emerson Street with its Maori koru fern leaf motif and zig-zags. I devour the beauty of these brightly coloured retro buildings against the bright blue sky. Contemporary wall art and graffiti compliments it all, with giant penguins standing behind tropical landscapes and a massive whale swimming out of a sardine can!

But if the truth be known, I'm exhausted. I find a supermarket, stock up on food, and simply hail down a taxi to take me back to the top of the hill. But the Indian driver, who's just moved here, doesn't know his way and drives miles out of town. I'm teetering to boiling point in anger with his incompetence and inadvertently show it in my tone of voice when I tell him to just leave me at the bottom of the hill. Although he tells me to calm down, he admits he didn't have a clue where he was going and insists on not charging me. I'm feeling abnormally stressed and put it down to tiredness. I guess one of the lessons for the day is that it can't be perfect all the time.

By the time I've dumped the food in the fridge and walked out to the back, my stress levels drop dramatically, as I'm about to have the most entertaining evening! Out on the terrace are two ladies, who introduce themselves in heavy German accents as Helga and Christa from Bavaria. For some strange reason, their two massive jam-packed suitcases are open and their worldly possessions dotted around, with clothes hanging from the sun loungers, chairs, and a little shed.

I look curiously at all the stuff. "Are you OK? You've just arrived? Yes?"

They both nod, and Helga, in tight shorts who looks like she's just come back from a marathon run, quickly interjects, "This is crazy! We've been put in this 'Summerhouse Shed' in the garden. When we arrived, the lady showed us this place and asked us to look inside. It is so squashed! Just enough room for one small bed and no room for our suitcases. I stamped out of the room and shook my head. 'Nein, nein nein; we can't accept this,' I told her. Then the lady says to me, 'Are you partners? It's nice and cozy!' I then screamed and said, 'Nein, nein, nein, just friends!' Then she leaves! What do we do?"

This is hilarious, and it's hard not to break out in friendly laughter. So as we later joke, the place had been mis-sold twice: for the lack of ease and access to park the bike, and secondly, a large spacious room for two innocent people! But even with both our difficult experiences today, we actually end up laughing about the ridiculous situation, happily make dinner together to eat on the terrace, and watch the setting sun while giggling all night with the help of one or two bottles of wine. It's amazing how things can change so quickly for the better.

4

Watch and Discover

Stings—Bad Eggs—Blue Baths—Gold Mines

The road leaving Napier opened up to wild marshlands and mountains with a railway line running alongside me on the ocean's side. I smile. The weather is dry. I'm initially planning to calmly head the 200 kilometres north-west up to Taupo. But already at 7:30 the speeding trucks are out making it feel like everyone is in a rush and making me feel dizzy!

But very shortly, in a blink of an eye, I'm on Route 5, or "The Thermal Explorer Highway." But that wasn't before making sure to fill the tank, as well as a spare litre petrol bottle I'd brought from the UK, as I'd been warned gas stations might soon become scarcer. The landscape was once again changing to beautiful hilly pasturelands. The weather was also warming up, and from the previous few days my chin had strangely got burnt and was now itching and peeling under the warm helmet. I needed to remove a layer. So at a fairly flat part of the road I pull over. Overlooking a field of horses contentedly grazing, I unzip my jacket. All of a sudden I feel a wasp fly into me and down my top. I become sick and dizzy from its sting on my shoulder and crazily flick away a spiky tail, which has got stuck in my skin. I sit down on the grass and try to breathe deeply, hoping it's not a poisonous tropical sting. I cross my fingers all will be well.

Feeling slightly better, I zip my jacket carefully back up, continue to ride further inland, and at Iwitahi, start entering massive areas of forests next to bare expanses of timber-cut land. These forests will be just the first of the many I encounter across the country. And at Taupo, overlooking the lake as I fill up, I notice it's a surprisingly big and moderately busy town with holiday homes and apartments dotted along the shoreline and covering smooth, green sloping hills very similar to back home. I continue northwards and am starting to register what a massive logging area this place is, with nearly every other vehicle a giant logger transporting the valuable wood.

After World War II, this area's economy boomed with farming, forestry, and tourism leading the way. It was an era of the most spectacular growth the region had ever seen. The population of Rotorua increased from 7,500 at the war's end to 46,000 in 1976, with the Kaingaroa Forest one of the largest man-made forests in the world.

But there was one stop I wanted to make before reaching Rotorua. Up a little road, I enter a carpark surrounded by forest with buses of gawping Chinese tourists rushing to an entrance gate.

This is Wai-O-Tapu (Sacred Waters), or Thermal Wonderland, and residing in one of the most active volcanic areas in the world. The Taupo Volcanic Zone is about 250 kilometres in length, stretching out to the Bay of Plenty. Well over a dozen massive craters are located here and were all formed by the surface collapsing with various types of geothermal activity, including steam fumaroles, sulphur vents, and bubbling, gurgling mud pools. Here the underground water system is so hot, with 300 degrees being recorded, that it absorbs minerals out of the rocks, transporting them to the surface as steam, and miraculously fills the craters with a multitude of different colours, from deep purple with the manganese oxide to bright yellow from the sulphur. It's an area of endless activity, and it's fascinating to see such exotic wonders surrounded by the oddly comforting landscapes of soft rolling hills and woodland that, once again, remind me of home. But I can't ignore the smell. The place stinks of rotten eggs, apparently from the hydrogen sulphide, so without further ado, I quickly leave.

Entering Rotorua and passing the lake with its Mississippi look-alike steamboat, I park up at the aptly-named Crash Palace Hostel. With a room all to myself, this'll do just nicely for a peaceful couple of days. But it's not until the next morning that I become worried. The sting on the shoulder has inflamed to become the size of a prize winning conker! It doesn't help, either, that directly under my right sole I've got a painful bump, also getting increasingly bigger. Reading on the Internet it truly or falsely claimed it may be a growth, which I'm trying to forget about. And not to forget when waking up, I discover other bumps all over my legs that I suspect are from bed bugs! It's suffocating in here, and I push open all five windows for air, which makes the black shutters sweep in the cool morning breeze and lets the sun shine onto the bed. But smelling the strong mineral air of the bad eggs reminds me in a macabre way that I need breakfast.

The temperatures are soaring, and predicted to reach 27C later in the day, as I walk along the road on my first mission to find a chemist. The white jacketed guy behind the counter couldn't be more helpful and reassures me that the "conker" is nothing to worry about and will slowly disappear and that New Zealand doesn't have poisonous wasps! I sigh with relief. However, he does look quizzical on the provenance of all the other bites I have and simply suggests I buy a pot of soothing cream from him!

Passing a couple of youths intertwined and snogging under the bus shelter, I sit outside the Artisan Café, witness the goings-on of the market vendors opposite me, and devour a "Sunshine Breakfast," promising myself to make the most of the day.

The flesh and blood Ghost Rider has also sent me a note—"By my reckoning you should be in New Zealand's capital of how to separate money from tourists city, Roto-Vegas. Don't worry if you miss out on soaking up some Maori culture here, because, don't fret, you are still coming up to Waitangi. Hopefully, the weather's good and the locals aren't fleecing you too much. You should be breezing up towards me tomorrow, so it'll be good to finally catch up for real and get a little bit of an interview done. I could come to you at Waihi, if that suits. It's not far from me, and I'll be road testing a new motorcycle. Just need your ETA. As to your request about meeting Hells Angels, I don't have a lot of contacts in this regard, but let me see what I can work out through a custom bike specialist. He may be able to point you in the right direction, if you're really set on travelling Chris Rea's Road to Angels, so to speak.

"We at *Bike Rider Magazine* tend to fraternise more with the Ulysses Club, which has the motto of 'growing old disgracefully' but doesn't have the overtly 'dodgy' nature of the H/A, Mongrel Mob, Highway 51, and the Headhunters. I can put you in touch with various Ulysses chapters, but these guys are choirboys by comparison with the Hells Angels.

"Just one last thing. How are you coping with our weird fuel? Should have mentioned this earlier. If you have some time, get hold of an app called Gaspy (Gas Spy). It can tell you where to find the best prices for fuel, which is usually Gull or Waitomo. I can educate you further tomorrow. Ciao Bella."

Without much persuading, I then go over to luxuriate at the heavenly Polynesian Pools. I sink into one of the warm natural pools looking out to the wild Lake Rotorua, watching birds fly overhead, before my Japanese masseuse, Miyuka, beckons me over. She bows politely, mysteriously providing a sachet labelled "Boy Leg." I snigger, but it's just a pair of disposable panties. Following suit I also bow, but she lets out a mouse-like giggle, shaking her head and saying, "No, no, no; that's too low and too deferential!"

From this calm sanctuary, I leave with a bouncy stride into a different world of street-lined commercial frenzy. The day is warming up nicely as I wander into the ornate rose lined gardens and towards the Elizabethan-style mansion built in 1908 as a bath house that provided treatments for the growing tourism industry. Until recently, it was the Museum of Art and History but has sadly closed for the foreseeable future, due to it falling well below earthquake safety standards. The good news is that it can be fixed, but all that depends on cost and time.

The park is filling up, and I'm hearing a multitude of languages and starting to agree when they say New Zealand is the meeting point for everyone. But I am noticing that growing numbers of modern Chinese tourists, now allowed to travel and with their massive amounts of disposable income, are very visible here. They're snapping away at literally everything, with one girl and a skirt up to her thighs positioning herself in every possible angle to take thousands of snaps of just the sunflowers. I'm also amused to even see miniature hot springs popping up in the park as I walk towards the Blue Baths.

This 1930s Mediterranean complex was one of the first public swimming pools in the world to offer mixed bathing. This outdoor pool is thermally heated, and I can't think of a better place to while away my afternoon. Walking in I hear a grand piano being played by Selwyn Wright as people politely sip their cups of tea and spread their scones with jam and cream. But it's surprising to see just a table of four enjoying the concert, and it's the same as I walk outside to the vintage pool, with only four polite children and their parents. So walking into the "Girls" changing room, I have this beautiful place almost to myself. It feels like a secret local haunt with just a few locals and no one reading *Lonely Planet*.

Later that afternoon, fully re-charged from the sun and swimming laps in the warm waters, I need to get practical and head back to the hostel to prep the bike for departure tomorrow. Out at the back, I kneel down and proceed to oil the chain. I look across and see a large seating area with at least fifteen other travellers, backpackers, and gap-year students solemnly looking into their cellphones and iPads. Not a word is being exchanged. Although together, they look isolated, creating their own invisible barriers. Are they running out to see the world around them or looking at it here from a screen? We're living in a generation where it seems nobody wants to be out of contact for long and is obsessed in being more "well-informed and prepped" than blindly spontaneous. Nobody curiously looks over to see what I'm doing, and it's just a bit deflating to witness this.

That evening, only really wanting a local corner shop, I have no other choice but to walk over to a giant outlet, just round the corner from the hostel, and walk miles down the aisles to stock up on food for tonight and for when I'm back out on the road. Sacks and boxes full of the same stuff were literally being pulled down from the shelves and heaved onto loaded trolleys. This is what I call a place for the serious shopper, and it reminded me that people were probably having to travel long distances from the countryside to stock up.

By the crack of dawn I'm on Route 33 riding towards the coast via Tauranga and Mt. Maunganui with the first blast through the kiwi fruit country of Te Puke (te Pookey). But no sooner have I left than I see more and more cars and trucks in my rear view mirror and up my arse! And here there are also the massive timber trucks to contend with. Overtaking is impossible or totally crazy. To say it as it is, there's no respite as they drive to almost touching point up and around the bends. This isn't enjoyable or relaxing, with no real places to stop on the sides of these steep and descending roads for rest or to even gawp at the views. Again, I'd go as far as to say that it's feeling dangerous, as everyone's in a rush. Thankfully, I've soon found a place to stop and down a strong coffee at the Te Puke Diner, better known as Kiwi Town, with its roads lined with tall conifer hedges protecting the kiwi fruit growing in the fields behind.

It's then riding over bridges and through the massive container port of Taurango on Highway 2 before stopping again on the other

side at Katikati for my first experience of one of New Zealand's staple foods, the famous pies. The little roadside shop has mouth-watering racks of freshly-baked, hot, golden, filled pastry delights; steak and cheese, sausage roll, butter chicken, steak and kidney, caramelized onion, steak and spinach, to name just a few. I grab a couple of the delicious pies, one for now and one stuffed in the tank bag for later back on the road.

Then it's a short run up to Waihi, where I'm glad to see I've arrived early at the Ti-Tree Café before Sean, my Ghost Rider, gets here. I park in front, out on Haszard Street, and go stretch my legs in this historical gold and silver mining township where the precious metals are still extracted. Up on the hill is the hollow concrete shell of the three-storey Cornish-style pumphouse that once extracted the water out just to keep the mine dry. Further up the road, I stop and peer almost 300 metres down into an abyss where massive dump trucks, looking more like the size of toys way down there, are working in the newer mines.

I look at my watch and turn back, curiously popping into an old church along the way where an art exhibition is being held, but it's strange to hear the handful of old women behind the stalls chatting with strong English accents! I walk over to the bike to check it's alright. From the corner of my eye, I notice a tattooed and dishevelled hobo slowly approach me and who curiously stops to look at the bike. He looks like he's high on drugs and slowly slurs, "Hey, quite a machine. I used to ride one in the day."

"Oh really?" I politely say, knowing I can run into the café.

"Yea, a long time ago … you know? … I used to live in a cemetery in Liverpool … I've got kids over there." He slowly strokes the tank and limps off.

I wander into the Ti-Tree. Sean's not here yet or I would have seen a bike parked up, so I walk to the counter to order a drink. Two guys waiting for their drinks see my helmet and nod their heads. "You riding round here?"

"Yes. Came up from Rotorua, but the roads are so busy!"

"We know! It's our holiday season, and until the beginning of Feb, the roads are crazy, particularly around here."

Walking into the back terrace towards me I see a smiling guy carrying a helmet, who I know without hesitation is Sean.

Over the next couple of hours, we have so much to talk about and catch up on, I don't want to forget to thank him for the amazing help he and Ghost Rider have already given me.

Sean bites into a muffin. "I know it's only the first part of your mega trip here, but how are the things panning out?"

I smile. "I'm really surprised at how British it is here. I try not to have too many, if any, expectations of what I'll find, but when I got to Christchurch I was amazed at how much like home it was, and that wasn't just there. I guess for most people who've never come here there is a sort of anticipation of a South Pacific island feel—the likes of which you've never seen before—you know, tropical beaches, exotic fruits, palm trees, that sort of thing. I'm sure I'm going to see some of that, but there's a lot more here that's sort of familiar. Of course, it's also very compact here. You can see and experience so much that's different, even in a day. I guess I wasn't ready for that either."

"Well, it'll be interesting to see your take of the upper North Island. But I've got to ask you, why did you select New Zealand as your next adventure? We live here, so we sort of take it for granted, and most kiwis have the natural instinct to get out and see the world, even if it's only Australia. Have you considered visiting the land of Big Red Rocks?"

"Australia's massive. I was looking for a destination that's eclectic and diverse, oh, and picturesque. Besides, New Zealand's a long way from home, and getting here was something of a challenging thing for me personally. Not knowing anything about the country made it just that much more appealing."

He nods, "Yea, but what's not so hot are our road manners."

"Yes, that's true. You're all so impatient to get to where you think you need to be, and the tailgating is actually quite frightening for a visitor, especially on two wheels. As a rider in this country, you really do have to have all senses on the ball. I've also noticed people here travel very closely to the centreline, so I've been probably a little too cautious in staying clear of it."

"You're right, and that's good. After we split, you'll be starting to ride up and around the Coromandel Loop. Riding the curves of the Coromandel can be a real challenge. I'd call it a pretty technical ride, which means the things that make it enjoyable also make it risky. You'll need to have your head in the game. Just make sure to take regular breaks; that'll enhance the enjoyment of the ride; and stay hydrated, as that helps you maintain focus. But the best safeguard is to always prepare. In the next few days of travelling look over your bike that it's in top order; best to plan your route before you leave each place; check the weather, as we've had issues there; and ride your own ride. Don't be influenced by others. That feeling of complete control can't be beaten."

I smile in total agreement. And he adds, smiling, "But don't worry too much, as your Ghost Rider buddy may just appear out on the road from time to time, providing some insight and support as you head north."

We walk out laughing, mount our bikes, and head out in different directions on our own roads.

5

Born to Be Wild

The Coromandel Loop—Shangri-La
Bike Gangs—Pig Man

Twisting and leaning round these sub-tropical luxuriant hills, I remember asking at the last gas station how far it was to Cooks Beach: "Oh, that'll be twenty or thirty minutes. We don't count miles here. It's too twisty! We've got difficult roads here and not for the faint hearted." So unsurprisingly and somewhat later than planned, I pull up next to a small boat on a trailer in front of a rainbow coloured fence.

In this quiet neighbourhood the engine must have alerted attention. A smiling, pretty woman with blonde pulled-back hair and traditional hand-tapped tattoos down her arms wanders up the garden pathway. She puts her hand out and shakes mine like she means business, but in a gentle voice says, "Welcome! I'm Kim, your host."

Then she looks at my luggage-packed bike, turns round towards the house, and putting two fingers in her mouth blasts out a deafening whistle. With that, I see eight smiling teenage boys amble up to take everything I've got.

"That's my son and his friends on summer vacation. Follow me. Your room's here, next to the garden. There's some fresh coffee, plums, oranges, and apricots from the garden; my homemade yoghurt, bread, and muesli I've just made; and some fresh eggs from our hens. I hope you're going to enjoy your time here! We'll have plenty of time to chat to get to know each other. Come up for a drink with us later when you're sorted and had a wander."

I sit down on the bed and breathe in the pretty details of everything around me, from the handpainted waves on the walls to an old metal bucket turned into a sink. I slip on my flip-flops and shorts and take a five-minute walk down the empty road to Cooks Beach. Every house in this silent place has a massive water tank, boat, and tractor in their front yard, which immediately illustrates the lifestyle here. Blue skies and wispy clouds float above as I reach the sandy white Cooks Beach and Mercury Bay. This is truly beautiful, and I'm speechless at its eclectic diversity. On one side are soft undulating wild sand dunes covered with beach grasses and tall pine trees, which wouldn't go amiss in the Southwest of France, across the bay are green tree-lined sloping hills looking out to sea and reminiscent of the Aberdyfi Beach in Wales, while out in the bay and standing alone are a number of green covered rock columns that you'd see in places like the

Phi-Phi Islands in Thailand. And I have the place all to myself, besides a few other people a lot further away paddling in the calm, rippling waters.

This special, remote place is named after James Cook, who effectively claimed New Zealand for King George III, planting the British flag at Cooks Beach in 1769. He spent twelve days anchored here, the longest he spent anywhere on his first voyage around Aotearoa. In observing the transit of Mercury across the sun on November 9 he was able to establish the exact latitude and longitude of the new-found land and renamed both these places Mercury Bay and Cooks Beach.

On the way back, I wander into a small shop to pick up some food. But the only fish in the freezer is fishing bait! It doesn't really matter, I'll be happy with simple food from the garden and some pasta from my bike. Later that evening, Kim shouts down and invites me up onto the terrace for a drink. This place really feels tropical.

"Hi there. We're drinking wine. Is that OK? Let me introduce you to my lovely husband, Terry."

A smiling, kind faced guy wearing a Rolling Stones T-shirt nods and passes me a glass. "Seen your transport. Looks good. I used to ride back in the '60s." Without any prompting he continues, "but drivers in New Zealand are crazy, speeding and going over lines. Even we let the cars and trucks go past us!"

I jolt, hearing a loud wolf whistle behind me, and Terry joins in with a laugh like an idling Harley-Davidson. "Hey, that's just our small talking parrots flying around in the kitchen. So what you wanna do while you're here? I'd stay put here if I was you."

"Well, I was reckoning on maybe taking a look over at Cathedral Cove."

He stops me immediately. "I wouldn't if I was you, as it's gonna be busy, but if you really wanna go I can drive you over tomorrow and pick you up later."

"That would be great and thanks, too, for all the food you put in my room."

Kim smiles. "Hey no problem. We're pretty self-sufficient here. We use the tank for the rain water we collect from the roof. We only have that to use and filtered to drink. It tastes great. We also even secretly take water from an underground well next door but where no one has lived for ages. And feel free to use anything growing in the garden. There're lots of herbs and seasonal veggies. All the flowers are edible too. That reminds me, if you're interested I'm gonna go scavenging for extra food tomorrow. You can come along. It's in this wild estate with just an old couple living at the top of its hill. There's food galore, which is never harvested and left to rot, so I don't really feel guilty, as I only take a small bit."

I smile eagerly nodding, "I'd love to help you. This place is great, and I'm so glad I'm staying with you guys for a few days."

More wine is poured, and Terry laughs again, "Yea we think so too—a bit off the radar, and I can tell you it's good. In the past I've travelled pretty much all over the place. I used to collect bulls' sperm worldwide and got to go to some fantastic places, but for us, this beats it all."

It's then I jump out of my seat and hear a non-stop wailing siren further up the hills. Taking a long casual swig, Terry continues, "We were told they were gonna just test it tonight, as we're in a Tsunami Risk and Evacuation Zone. There's stuff in your room about it, but if we think one is coming we'll need to get to higher ground or rush inland. There're also natural warnings that appear if a Tsunami is arriving here on the coast. You might feel a strong earthquake like it's hard to stand up or feel a weak one that lasts for a minute or more. You might also see strange sea behaviour, such as the level suddenly rising or falling, and the sea will make loud and unusual noises or roar like a jet engine. We may only have minutes to act before it arrives and are told to take a battery powered radio for news and to wait for the official all-clear before returning. New Zealand's entire coast is at risk, and tsunamis can occur anytime of the year with a massive destructive force travelling over land, picking up debris, boats, and knocking down buildings!"

Early next morning, it's drizzling as Kim and I jump into the jeep, throwing bags in the back and feeling like we're on a secret military operation.

Kim definitely speaks like she knows what she's doing, "OK, when we get there, I'll park just up the road to hide the jeep, and then we'll walk back and clamber over the gate. Just don't make any noise!"

So with bags in hand I nervously follow Kim over the gate and into a wild Shangri-La of majestic tropical vegetation and macrocarpa cypress trees that lead into an enormous secret garden. Vegetable plots are overflowing with corn and beans, and trees and shrubs bursting with grapefruit, apricots, plums, lemons, feijoa, avocados, apples, pears, figs, and blueberries.

Kim's already foraging around, "Quick, let's pick up stuff mostly from the ground that's still good enough to eat so we're not really taking the best. This'll do us for the next few days. The couple, they're old, live at the top, and won't see us through the forest."

We continue to tip-toe around, filling our bags until we've no more room.

"Before we go, I want to show you a really special place here. It's a massive waterfall and pond where I sometimes go to swim."

Through the ancient trees, bamboo, and fern we come to a magical high cliff of rock and moss where silver water comes tumbling down. We each sit on a big rock at the edge.

"I've never seen such a hidden, mystical place that you'd call a back garden. This place just exudes peace."

"Yea, I come here sometimes just for the good vibe. I've gone through a lot in life to get to where I'm fortunate to be now. I used to live in Hawaii and got introduced by a boyfriend to heroin and became addicted. I was needing to find $500 a day for it, so started stealing and got me into prison. Just that nightmare forced me to stop and turn my life around. At the beginning here, I used to own an ice-cream parlour down on the beach. Boy, that was fun but hard work. We did crazy things like offer six balls of ice cream scooped into one cone! I would sell 280 lbs. of ice-cream in a day! I've come from a family who worked hard. My mum lives down the road from me, and boy, does she have stories! She used to run and own an airport close to Los Angeles. You'll have to meet her on the way back. We live simply here and try to survive from the land—you know, 'stolen fruit' from neighbours gardens tastes even better! In reality, I'd love to build an 'Earth Ship' to be totally self-sufficient! Yes, I love our place and have designed and built a lot of it.

"But the majority of places around here are second homes owned by a lot of wankers and empty most of the time, so there's not much community spirit. A lot of the people here have that island mentality, thinking they're better than anyone else and they also don't like to see others succeed, which we call here the Crab Pot Theory. But I don't give a shit; we're doing just fine."

With that, we scamper like naughty kids through the trees, climb over another fence and into an orchard to grab another handful of plums before racing off. I'm smiling from ear to ear with the thrill of it all.

Kim's mother, Jill, opens the door, noticing our sticky plum coloured hands and waves us in to wash them. This is another strong outspoken woman who proudly shows us an idyllic oil canvas she's just completed of Cathedral Cove.

During our cup of tea she slips back into time—"It was the beginning of summer, 1946, and it was to be the first time that we came to camp at Hahei Beach on the Coromandel. My father had walked out of a construction site in downtown Auckland, and a plank was accidentally dropped, landing on his head. He was advised he must have total rest and no stress for a period of time.

"It was suggested to my mother, by the manager of Whitcombe and Tombs where she had worked as a girl, that we should have a holiday at Hahei. He had just come back from there, seeing it while on a trip with a staff member of AA. The camping equipment and most of our supplies were to be brought down by boat from Auckland to Ferry Landing at Whitianga and then around to Hahei after the Harsants, who owned the farm, were advised the boat would be coming. We left Auckland early in the morning in the 'big black car' (Austin early 1930s). It was to be a long journey. We made our first stop at Kawakawa Bay for Dad to stretch his legs and make a contact with a Maori elder, whom he was acquainted with, by the name of Turei, he was known to be one of the last celestial navigators. Back in the car and on around the coast to Pipiroa. There was no bridge built over the Pipiroa River. You crossed it on a wooden planked barge winched by cable. The car was driven onto the barge and winched to the other side, then it came back and transported us across. The Kopu Bridge, called the Hauraki Bridge then, had been built over the Waihou River in 1928, and it was quite a novelty, as it was the only single-lane swing bridge in New Zealand. No signal lights, just passing bays. Fortunately there was no 'road rage' in those days, and occasionally there would be livestock crossing on it as well.

"It seemed to take forever coming around the Thames coast on a very narrow, windy gravel road making us ask, 'Are we there yet?' We stopped under the huge pohutukawa trees at Tapu for a picnic lunch and, of course, to check the water in the radiator. We had also made a stop while in Grahamstown (Thames) at the 4 Square Grocery Store, owned by the Woods family, where mother had placed an order to come down to the farm. I believe that the orders were brought by truck over the hill to Coroglen, where they were picked up and brought down to the farm in empty cream cans coming back from the Dairy Co-op in Whitianga.

"The drive over the Tapu Hill (only fifteen miles) was slow and dusty. The road was nothing more than a 'bullock track,' big sized white rock and really only one vehicle wide. There were very few passing bays. All the windows down, with dust billowing in, we all had to sit in total silence so Dad could hear any sounds of traffic. Every sharp bend he would sound the horn, and you would hear it echoing around the bend. The bush was thick, and it all had a *Jurassic Park* effect. Nowhere to stop until the summit, check the water in the radiator, a 'Mrs. Murphy' stop, a drink, thankfully nobody was car sick, then a slow drive, winding down the other side of the ranges, past the big Kauri tree, into the valley and on in to Coroglen.

"The Pub at Coroglen was a small shed; it is still there; stop, out of the car, dusty, hot and thirsty. A shandy for Mum, beer for Dad, and sarsaparilla all round for the children. Oh, did I hate sarsaparilla, still do; I just wanted a lemonade.

"Over the newly built bridge and past the Gumtown Hall, from then on we were on very poor roads, built mostly of clay with a little gravel, to the turn off at Dalmeny Corner and then to now what is the Cooks Beach turn off, which was the original road to Hahei. Relief workers, employed by the government during the depression years, did most of the road works. No machinery, all done with pick and shovel and steel rimmed wheelbarrows. There were a couple of quarries around the area of Cooks Beach. Every river ford required a stop, and out would come the hammer to pound in all the nails that would be sticking up out of the few planks and a good look at the level of the stream.

"It was late afternoon when we arrived, and what a thrill it was coming over the ridge for that first glimpse of that dazzling view of sparkling turquoise blue sea and the necklace of islands out from the beach; it was magic. The original road did not go through the small gorge that is there now; it just came right over the top. Stop to open farm gates, a breathtaking view, bumping down through the paddock track to 'the cottage.' Both Horace and Florence were there to greet us.

"We arrived to find the camping equipment had been rowed ashore on to the beach, at the north end, where the two big pohutukawa trees are. However, they forgot to unload the tent poles off the scow. A farm person was put on a horse to ride over to Ferry Landing to be there when the boat came round to tell them they would have to come back with the poles. They didn't come back till the next day, so that night we stayed in the 'big house.'"

With that Jill smiles and leans back, I'm sure reflecting on those good times.

That afternoon Terry kindly drives me to a drop off point where I can walk over and down the hills to Cathedral Cove.

Along the way, the views out to sea are spectacular, but it's not the first time I encounter disappointment. The little beach is jam packed with shorts and costume-clad people taking pictures left, right, and centre. It's impossible for me to see, even for one moment, the empty archway. I don't really want to spend a moment longer and so quickly leave, agreeing with Kim and Terry that there's no need to really step far from Cooks Beach. I have it all there with the most wonderful, genuine people.

A few days later, after another "up and down" hilly bending series of roads through tropical forests, pine forests, fields of Herefords, and riding thankfully against the holiday traffic, I'm stoked to arrive at the charming little harbour town of Coromandel and Anchor Lodge.

Chuck, the Filipino receptionist, who's proudly just got his working visa through sponsors here at the motel, politely shows me to the dorm. It's a scene of chaos, with five double bunkbeds for ten people with their bags and crap all over the place. I shake my head to him and walk out. I'm not going to be happy here for three nights! He smiles understandingly and walks me to the last available cabin, ironically called "Last Resort," overlooking the green fields leading to the estuary inlets and boating pontoons. This time I nod my head, shake his hand, and put the extra dollars in his other one.

"There're quite a few things to see here, but next to your lodge there's an old gold mine tunnel. Help yourself to our gum boots when it gets darker, and you might have a nice surprise."

So after a long walk to Long Bay Beach, or what looked more like "campervan village," the tide has turned and the muddy mangrove tributaries through the estuary have filled up with the boats no longer stuck in mud but bobbing around. On my way back a truck turns off from the fishing boat pontoon advertising on its side "Fin Fish—Blue Abalone—Wild Abalone—Lobster—Oyster," which reminds me I need to buy a few supplies from town. With the sun slowly setting, I'm soon out on my porch with my feet up on a chair, contentedly gazing at the bike parked right next to me while eating some of the delicious local fish.

In the pitch dark, I pull on the rubber gum boots and carrying the lantern, walk the few metres into a muddy, wet, lined tunnel entering the rock face. Without seeing much more than a few feet in front of me, I cautiously continue walking and sliding along the tunnel, which disappears out in front. Without exaggeration it's quite scary, but what I'm now seeing are, like stars, progressively increasing numbers of bright lights flickering on the roof and cave walls all around me until the place becomes totally covered with these sparkling delights. Tripping from time to time, due to the slippery mud, I stop and squint all around me in this dark, silent world, where all I can now see around me are the flashing, sparkling glow worms.

I head back, and tired from the day, finally switch the cabin lights off and turn over to sleep. But not for long! The bright light of a headlight sweeps across my curtains as I hear the roaring of motorbike engines. Then there's silence again, and I drop off.

As I go to leave the gumboots at reception the next morning, the owners son, Regan, stands up to take them from me. "Hopefully you weren't disturbed too much last night. It was one of the 'Head Hunters' chapters who rode in with a car full of girls, but they've already split for the coast."

He can see I'm interested. "They're one of the outlaw motorcycle clubs, with the Hells Angels as allies. They've got quite a criminal history dealing with drugs and money laundering, but I guess if you don't get involved, you're fine."

I was later shocked to learn from a recent interview in a paper from Detective Sergeant Craig Martin Turley that this was true: "They're considered one of the most dangerous criminal operations in the country. They control the West Auckland crime scene, responsible for the sales, manufacturing and distribution of all class drugs with deals taking place across the country. Their organized theft and distribution of stolen property has a value, over the years, in the millions."

Regan's on a roll, "And if you wanna hear some other interesting stories, go and have a chat with my friend, 'Johnny.' He's quite a character." I swallow hard, as I wasn't expecting such excitement so early in the day, but curiosity gets the better of me and I wander down the quiet little street to try and find "Johnny." I come across a dishevelled guy with a skull tattoo on his shoulder mowing a lawn in a quaint little cottage.

Without removing his dark glasses so I can't see his eyes, he murmurs, "You're too early. I haven't got the place ready yet."

"No, no, no!" I reassure him, "I'm not coming to stay. It was just that Regan mentioned you. I'm travelling around, getting some stories. You know? We had the Head Hunters come in last night!"

He smiles in more of a relaxed way from what I've just said and leads me to the terrace, where he drops himself down into a wicker chair, rolls a cigarette, and kicks his jandals off. "Yea. I know. There's more than a few in jail for murder mostly, East Auckland. The police recently seized six million dollars of their assets because of drugs."

And like that, without any prompting, for the next hour I listen to the most bizarre one-sided jumpy conversations from this guy who doesn't know me from Adam, about everything and nothing, but mainly about sex, drugs, and rock'n'roll!

"Well, first of all, I have to say you only look like you're in your late thirties. Shit! No? Really?! So how are you affording this trip? You gotta get a sugar daddy! I've got a sugar mummy. They'll just want to see you three or four times a year. Then they die and you get the dollars! But yea, I've spent a lot of time in Australia doing cross terrain biking stuff. Done Pat Pong Bangkok. You into drugs? Ever taken them? Nothing in Cambodia. I've just been around the world. In Los Angeles I met one of the girls through WhatsApp. She was in the Carolinas. I stayed there eight weeks. Yea, and back in LA there's a funny story. I went up to see an old guy in Frisco, as I hadn't heard from him and thought he'd been shot. I told my friend that if I didn't return to call the FBI! I got there, and he'd just turned all his stuff off."

I'm discreetly looking over his shoulder to the wall clock inside while he's looking me up and down, and I feel we need to maybe shorten this encounter. But he goes on, "This place here I've got is crazy. Makes me good money. I normally charge just a couple of hundred or so, but one weekend I already had friends staying so had nothing to lose when an American couple turned up, and, just for fun, I asked $800! And you know what? They accepted and said I'd saved their skin. Now that's crazy man!"

I smile and get up to leave, thanking him for such an interesting time, and he can't help but ad, "Now you remember, come back for a drink or whatever later, and we can continue."

My steps back are a little quicker than normal, but I smile at the openness of this kind stranger before grabbing a bicycle from the motel and quickly peddle in the opposite direction up to Driving Creek Railway. Along the way, my grin becomes even broader as I pass a fence totally covered with jandals, or flip-flops to us Brits, of every size and colour and one of New Zealand's iconic lifestyle symbols. In 1956, the Japanese swimming team were observed wearing a new type of casual footwear at the Melbourne Olympics. Around the same time, an Auckland businessman saw similar versions of traditional thongs in Asia and was determined to introduce the idea to New Zealand.

A little sweaty from the cycle up the hill's steep incline, I'm soon immersed in another amazing world of the late Barry Bricknell by riding his little train up through the mountains.

A Ronnie Wood lookalike driver welcomes us, "So, hello everyone. Barry became New Zealand's first full-time potter. He managed to buy this sixty-acre place in '73 for $8,000. His vision, with nothing on the property, just a little bit of bush, was to build a pottery where artists from all over the world could work and live for a while. And to also build a fifteen-inch narrow-gauge railway just to get the clay and firewood down to the potteries and at the same time replant everywhere with natural trees. But people started hearing a train and came up asking for rides, so he decided to build an old carriage behind his old work engine. He simply put a donation box on it, and that helped him build the track all the way to the top. He collected rail lines from all the old coal mines in Waikato, everything done by himself and with a lot of wine drunk to finish it! Over there you'll see lots of silver fern, and like the natives here, we'd turn them over if we were in the bush to remember the track or even be found!"

Along the way, we pass quirky pottery sculptures and artworks until we reach the observatory point at the top with a sight for sore eyes looking out over the 360 degrees across the undulating countryside and sea. It's quite an engineering feat, with Barry passing away in 2016, leaving his crazy buddies to continue building the trains here.

The cycle back to the lodge is an easy one as I whiz, without peddling, helter-skelter down the hill. I'm back on the bicycle the next day but riding in the opposite direction out of town for a few miles to the 309 Road. This is New Zealand's famous scenic twenty kilometre journey, which crosses the backbone of the Coromandel Peninsula. It's mostly unsealed, showcasing spectacular scenery

as it winds through farmland, pine forests, and native bush. I'll see how far I can peddle! So far, so good, as it's pretty flat. At the corner of SH25 and 309 Road I stumble across the highly praised Coromandel Mussel Kitchen, which motivates me to get back safely later for a well-deserved pot of juicy mussels.

For a mile or so it's still asphalt, but the roads are curving slowly round and upwards into wild bush. Around the corner and a little further on, I see what looks like a small farmstead, but the closer I get the more amazed I become in what I've found. In the middle of this remote area is a sandy, rubbly patch of land with a handful of old decrepit and decaying cars and vans, but also full of pigs of every size and colour with crowing cockerels to add to the mix. And standing in the middle of all the pigs is a barefooted, white-haired man silently feeding them. I have to stop. With all this cycling my foot with the bump under it is sore, and I limp slightly over to the barbed wire fence to take a closer look and a rest.

A cleaner looking and taller by a foot guy, but wearing the same tartan shirt, approaches carrying a little black piglet in his arms.

I smile and the same is reciprocated back. "This little one got under the wire, and I had to go and chase him. We've got poachers here. Some put food down along the road to tempt them out."

"Oh," I reply, sounding interested, and point over to the guy on the other side of the fence, "Who's feeding them?"

"Well that's my brother, Stu, and I'm Jim. I live in the farmhouse over there up the hill, but Stu spends most of his time living here with the wild pigs."

I nod, "And so what do you do?"

"Well, besides working on the farm, I find water with my hands and dowsing sticks and then drill it. I recently found one on some land nearby that was giving a hundred litres a second!"

I stand back in wonder. This isn't a normal, everyday kind of person. With that, to show me there's water underneath, he then kneels down, lays his hands over a spot of the land, and his hands immediately start to shake as he tells me they feel like they're burning. He rests his hands on mine and asks if I can feel anything, which frustratingly, but maybe not surprisingly, I don't!

He continues stroking his pig. "I also saw you limp over a bit. Are you alright?"

I mention the worry about the limp and that the lump under my foot seems to be getting bigger and more painful. He nods and, without asking me anything else, seems to all of a sudden go into a trance. He lets go of the piglet. His strong hands start to shiver and shake as he sweeps them around and over me while pushing them together and away like he's frantically grabbing, pushing, and clearing something horrible away. It truly looks tiring hard work. I remain still until he's finished and he opens his eyes.

Almost out of breath he says, "I think I've cleared something and pulled out the negative energy from you! I can also heal people from distances. I travel around quite a bit. It's because I see ghosts everywhere, mainly Maori who've been killed, and I'm asked to help 'move them on' from where they've been massacred! I help the spirits pass on from here. I remember one Maori ghost drove in the car with me up to the north, and an old lady on the way saw the same ghost with me too! Some time back, I started to see them when I was just four years old, but I never said anything, thinking my family would think I was crazy. I also see my wife's spirit, who passed away."

All I can do is solemnly nod, but his stories captivate me, and I somehow believe every word he's passionately saying.

He breathes in deeply, and maybe now speaking more to himself says, "I don't know why I was chosen to do all this healing work. And it's terrible what's happened with my family. My wife died last year. They've been destroyed by the neurologists in the local hospital, and my daughter is now crazy with only half a brain, and the CEO took $50,000 for holidays. Crooks! But we have to continue to help, don't we? Where are you heading next?"

I quietly and respectfully reply, "I'll be heading up to the very north."

Jim bends down and picks up the piglet. "I have a nice ten-acre place and big barn up there where we paid just $105K! Well, you're more than welcome to stay at my place up there if you want, and of course, free of charge."

I smile at Jim's genuine generosity and shake his hand without aiding the piglet to escape. And wobbling just a little from the stories I've just heard, I cycle quickly back down to Mussel Kitchen.

6

Beach Heaven

Auckland Mayhem—Lions Head
Pohutukawa—Bach

The bike's been given a quick look over, my waterproofs are pulled over my ever thickening layers, and I head out onto Route 25, closely hugging the coastline through and over the undulating hills. There's no denying the fact that it's miserably cold, with a dense mist floating out to sea and heavy ominous black clouds following me with increasingly strong winds.

I'd received a note earlier from Sean confirming my suspicions, "Yep made it back. Great seeing you. That Harley's not bad once you get used to sitting like Cool Hand Luke and walking bow legged for the rest of the day! Anyway, I reckon you'll be heading into Thames today and don't forget you have to declare any glowworms you've smuggled out of Coromandel. It's going to be a big ride if you're staying on schedule. Be careful. By my calculation you're looking at four plus hours of road time and around maybe 250 kilometres to Beach Haven, and that's assuming light traffic in Auckland!

"There's been some storm issues on the road recently, so be mindful of slips, not the petticoat kind, and roadworks. The Hauraki council is not as flush financially as the national government so work won't be as fast as it was for Kaikoura. See how it goes but you've two options. Either the Seabird Coast where the Dotterels come to New Zealand for the winter and then the little buggers migrate back to Europe. Or you can simply take Highways 2 and 1 as you probably just want to get to Beach Haven with the least amount of city stress. Plenty of time to stress later.

"And remember, culturally sensitive as we are, Kiwis don't think Asians can drive, so a little caution at intersections, roundabouts, car parks oh heck, anywhere there's a car really!"

He was right, forecasts today had stated that heavy rain may cause streams and rivers to rise rapidly, surface flooding was possible, and driving conditions would be hazardous with a massive storm predicted to come into the Auckland area later in the day.

Just outside Thames, at Thornton Bay, important road works are still being done to bravely clear the rubble caused by the higher than average sea levels that came unexpectedly flooding in from the storms the day I arrived in New Zealand. So in convoy, through the wet rubble and debris laden sea hugging road, we're slowly escorted by a truck with a flashing "keep left" sign. Now this is scary, and my speed drops dramatically, just hoping the bike won't slip over. A hot brew in Thames comforts me somewhat as I start to re-plan the route to get to Auckland. My gut says I need to get there as soon as possible, keep away from the stormy coast and head inland for better safety, and avoid any loitering.

Jumping onto the bike, an old man being knocked sideways by the wind approaches and, holding onto his hat, yells out, "That's a great bike; reminds me of the good old days." And with that, he waves me off.

I join Route 25 at Waitakaruru, then it's all the way to Auckland, over the famous but blustery Harbour Bridge looking over the city, and glance down to my hand, where I'd simply written my instructions: "Beach Haven—Exit 422—Stafford Road." With just a few stops and starts to check the route, I finally pull into a house's driveway at the end of a long residential road and sigh, turning the engine off.

A small guy in even smaller shorts comes running over to me shouting in a strong French accent, "Bonjour! I'm Patrick your host. Now look here, non, non, non this won't do! I suggest you move your bike out of sight behind my hedge. I used to be a biker, and there're gangs in the neighbourhood who might take it! And oh, mon dieu, there's a massive storm predicted to arrive tonight, so make sure you get food at the New World Supermarket in Chatsworth before it comes in! I also have two Dutch ladies arriving in their campervan, so we need to make more space! Sacrebleu!"

I'm surprised by his melodramatic flourish but smile and dutifully obey. Later on, looking out over the beautiful picturesque terrace with rain pelting down across the bay, I text Debra, the South African biker I'd met on the boat coming over, that I'd arrived. She enthusiastically suggests we meet in Auckland's downtown district tomorrow.

But I'm just a little nervous to take the bike into Auckland tomorrow, not only because of the weather but also remembering a note a British friend had recently sent me of a letter he'd sent to his brother about his journeys by bicycle through the city. And that was ten years ago! I don't know whether to laugh or weep …

"2009—Riding a bicycle in Auckland is the quickest way to death or injury. We have lots of Asian drivers here and they don't care about anything that's happening outside their own personal space, which extends about as far as their washer jets. They are responsible for more accidents than anything else.

"Then there are the boy racers who will actually target cyclists and lastly the bus and truck drivers who don't really care because cyclists bounce off and don't do any real damage to the vehicle. Together they even managed to kill a senior police officer whilst he was leisure riding his bike and who was, ironically, in charge of Road Safety for the whole country. There are cycle lanes, but other road users consider them an extra extension to the width of the road and drive in them anyway. You really have no idea what it is like to drive here.

"Overtaking on the left on motorways is legal. Indicators are optional (so it seems). On motorways they don't take any account of the approaching speed of cars in the lane they intend to move to. Lots of surprise braking goes on. They also have no idea what to do with a roundabout, i.e. to turn right, drive all the way round in the left lane, then you don't have to change lanes before turning off. They widened the motorway by adding two feet to it and then painted the lanes narrower and hey presto another lane! There are no countdown markers to motorways or main road turnoffs. So you go barrelling along and round a slight curve, suddenly there is the exit! Oh yes and here in Auckland at traffic lights you suddenly find that the 'Straight On' lane that you were in, is now 'Turn Left Only' because the arrows painted on the road were covered up by the car in front, but it's too late to get out of it. No signs by the side of the road or anything helpful like that. You certainly get to see some unexpected parts of the city. You starting to get the picture?"

The 973 bus's windscreen wipers are working overtime as we cross the misty, cloud-laden Auckland Harbour Bridge with little or no visibility over to the downtown area and the ferry terminals. The half-hour ride has cost me just $5.50 and avoided me riding frantically in the rain, trying to find my way plus somewhere to park. Travel doesn't always have to be difficult, and I'm starting to want it as easy as possible!

Similar to the first day in Christchurch, I walk through heavy rain and puddled streets, holding tightly onto an umbrella. At "Best Ugly Bagels" in York Street, while tucking into an avocado and bacon toasted bagel, I take my shoes off and put them next to the radiator to somewhat dry, hoping the downpour will stop.

It doesn't, so I rush over to the Auckland Art Gallery in Albert Park, this time for some cultural nourishment. I'm delighted to see Marti Friedlander's photography of an earlier, more innocent New Zealand in the 1950s and iconic Charles F. Goldie's incredible paintings of the early 1900s depicting Maori and Pakeha tribe leaders with their heavily adorned Moko fascial tattoos. These paintings are enduring taonga (treasures) and connections to a not-so-distant past.

Gazing up to the iconic Sky Tower with its top half now hidden in clouds, the wind suddenly comes from around a high rise building and blows my umbrella inside out, making it totally useless, and I have no other choice but to dump it into a garbage bin. I run back to the waterfront and patiently wait on the wharf outside the National Maritime Museum, where the rain finally decides to stop. Before long, I recognise the laughing face and waving hand of Debra driving towards me and careering to a shuddering halt, with a small boy seat belted in the back.

Also speaking just as quickly, "Hey Zoë, I can't believe we've hooked up. This is my son, Alf. I just gotta drop something off at the office and then we wanna show you round a bit."

With that, I get in next to her, and she pushes her foot down and accelerates off at speed. Before long, we're driving back over the bridge. "I don't know what you're doing over the next few days, but Leon and I thought that at the weekend we could take a longer jaunt and drive out on the west coast for you to see some of the places there and stop to chill out on the beach at Piha.

But today I thought we'd drive over to the posh part, to Devonport, where we also used to live. It's on the north shore overlooking Auckland, and it's where the rich commuters live."

I'm in total agreement with the plan. This couldn't be better. We park up at beautiful Devonport and walk into a bar overlooking the harbour and ferry terminal. The views are spectacular as the constant flow of commuter ferries come in and out.

This is a party girl, and we can't stop laughing as she walks around the bar to serve us two big glasses of wine and a cola for her son, while I threaten to spray her with some soda!

We click our glasses together. "You can smell the wealth here. Look at those shiny big cars driving past and those prettily dressed women walking into those tea rooms over there on Queens Parade." She then looks at her watch. "We gotta go now before rush hour hits, but as you know, we're just down the road from you so we'll pick you up on Saturday. And don't forget your cossie! Tomorrow I'm sure you'll have fun exploring the cliff walks or just chilling by your pool."

By Saturday morning the storm's thankfully disappeared as I sit drinking coffee and flicking through the *Weekend Herald* on the terrace waiting for the guys to arrive. The headlines are big! "An historic first baby. New Zealand rejoices with Prime Minister Jacinda Ardern and her partner Clarke Gayford as they announce an 'unexpected surprise' She's set to make her mark in history again, as the first New Zealand Prime Minister to give birth in office— and just the second in the world. Ardern says that after becoming Labour leader in August, they'd put baby plans on hold but as it turned out, nature had other plans!"

A car's horn honks outside, and grabbing my bag, I run up the driveway to be greeted by three smiling faces as I jump into the back.

Debra's even more excited and is talking nineteen to the dozen. "We haven't got much time, I know. But we want to show you as much as possible and why we love this place. We wanna take you out on the 'Scenic Drive' of Route 24 to Arataki Visitor Centre, where you'll see incredible views out to the Tasman Sea, and then we'll head down to Piha."

And true to her word, climbing through the Waitakere Ranges Regional Park, the views out to sea are spectacular. A bit further on, the coastal view from the lookout above Piha Beach is just as dramatic, but a familiar image for New Zealanders. High above the beach, generations of surfers have stopped here to check the waves before descending down the steep road to the sea. Standing sentinel on the beach is Lion Rock, the colossal island fortress of the ancient Maori, known as Whakaari, and known by generations of Kiwis as one of the most famous coastal landmarks in the country. Every summer Piha Beach becomes a magnet for serious surfers and a temporary home for thousands. It's the most popular west coast beach in New Zealand, with its surf always living up to expectations.

Today we're lucky, as it's not too busy, except for some avid surfers and the yellow and red clad lifeguards patrolling the beach. We kick our shoes off and walk along the fine sandy beach watching the surfers' skills out on the waves. "Wow, the sand is so black, it looks almost volcanic!"

Leon smiles, "It is. It's the ashes!"

Then it's an afternoon simply lazing on this iconic beach and tucking into our picnic. The day rushes by, but not before we've driven the forty kilometres and walked down to the Karekare Waterfalls for a quick toe dip. Driving back towards Auckland it feels busy, and Leon seems to know what I'm thinking and smiles stating, "Yea, it's not getting any better. Apparently 800 cars are being newly registered each week due to the population explosion here in Auckland. I know you're leaving tomorrow on a Sunday, but just be careful."

Big hugs are given all around as I'm dropped off, and I wave goodbye to these kindest of people who just happen to also ride bikes!

With just over a hundred kilometres to cover the following day, and fortunately riding against traffic coming into Auckland, after passing through the Hibiscus Highway, I make a small detour off the busy dual carriageway to historic Puhoi village. It's a tiny place, once home to Catholic Bohemian migrants who arrived in 1863 making a living from the poor land by cutting the bush for timber. I'd also been told more than once that this was home to the Puhoi Tavern, famous for welcoming bikers from all over the place. But the welcoming breakfast I'd been looking forward to is off, as the white timber colonial inn is closed on this quiet Sunday morning.

So sitting next to the bike on the pavement in front of the Puhoi Trading Post I carefully re-read the instructions from Sharley from the Pakiri Beach Stables: "If you're coming from Wellsford or Matakana, roads are sealed all the way except for the last 3kms coming to us. But even the Rahuikiri road has good surfaces for bikes. I should know, my husband had a Bonneville!"

Without much else to see around here, I start the bike up and pass the tiny telephone box-like Puhoi Town Library, with its stacks of books and honesty box on the pavement, and unsuccessfully try to leave quietly without disturbing the peace of this little place too much.

Although it's not far to travel today, I'd chosen Pakiri Beach for its isolation, knowing all too well there wouldn't be much going on. For the next couple of days I'd just be living simply in a little bach among the sand dunes and maybe, just maybe, I'd go galloping with horses along the wild beaches. So on this warm but grey, cloudy morning the bike and I contentedly accelerate off, turn right at Warkworth, and continue to the intersection at Matakana, a pretty, little affluent settlement. It feels more like a place you'd see in The Hamptons on Long Island, with a children's gymkhana taking place in Jubilee Park with rosetted ponies trotting round the obstacle laden field with proud parents looking on. It's also here I stop off to stock up with food and fill the tank, knowing there'll be nothing where I'm going. It's beautiful riding past green fields bordered with leafy trees, and at this moment in time, there's not a single other person out on these quiet roads.

At a small T-junction, a sign tells me to turn right to Pakiri Beach. I stop close by, noticing a woman walking out onto the road to check her letterbox, and walking towards her I nod to say hello. It's here I see the road has now turned to, and what will be my first experience of riding, a non-sealed track of road. I breathe deeply and get back on. Now before I start, I'm not giving excuses, but I'm nervous as I slowly ride with this enormous weight, feeling it just doesn't seem to be as agile or stable on this rough gravelly road. For the next two miles and from time to time I'm putting my feet on this awkward ground to just re-stabilize everything from sliding over, knowing all the time I won't be able to pick it up. So along this, thankfully, flat track I go at my own slow pace, and although it's not a total nightmare, it is unsettling and I arrive at the stable block sweating slightly.

A smiling bloke in cut-off jeans and a pastry brush in one hand, waves and walks over. "Hi, I'm Tim who runs the café here. Sharley mentioned you were coming, but they're out on a ride at the moment. Love that bike! Do a bit myself. But do you reckon you can ride it up the sand track and over some grassy dunes to the bach? Or do you want me to take you and your gear in my four-wheeler?"

I've stopped breathing so deeply and smile with relief, "Great to meet you. This place is crazy, so remote, with just these stables, your café, and a few cattle grazing in the fields. You're kind, if it doesn't put you out, but yes, I might just take you up on your offer and leave the bike here on flat ground."

He nods in agreement, "Yea, we like it here. Let me drop you off. You ain't seen nothing yet, on the other side out to sea!"

So with Tim at the wheel, and the bags thrown in the back, he drives his big four-wheel jeep up a rough road, bumping up and through slippery sand dunes leading to a little grassy area sheltered by trees where a small black wood cabin, or bach, appears. I'm excited. This is literally in the back of beyond, and I'm now starting to hear the sound of crashing waves from the other side of the sandy mounds.

"So how do you like this place? Walk down to the café if you need any milk or anything, and Sharley had said she'll get you organised for riding out tomorrow. You might hear some strange noises at night, but there's nothing to be frightened of; it's all nature and it's all safe. Oh yea, just one thing when you get to the sea. Sure you can take a swim if you want, and if it's warm enough, but if you get caught up in a rip tide just 'go with it' and don't swim against it."

With that, Tim helps me unload everything and I walk up the few wooden steps and see the bach's name "Pohutukawa" nailed on the wall, with the same red-flowered trees and their twisted trunks and roots behind it.

He smiles, "Given the farthest you can ever be from the sea in New Zealand is only something like 130 kilometres and that the majority of us live little more than 10 kilometres from the coast, then it's only natural the beach plays such a big part of our lives. So it's no wonder that the summer holidays see a lemming-like migration from our cities and towns. So like migratory birds, we make temporary homes in tents, caravans, and bachs. For a society already greatly egalitarian, the beach is the final levelling, where labourers and executives, farming folk and townies blend in a confusion of jandals, shorts, and T-shirts.

"And symbolic of the beach and coasts here is the pohutukawa tree representing our summer. It thrives on the salt spray and can grow in really difficult spots and mostly found here in the upper North Island."

With that, he waves goodbye and rattles back down the track. Inside the bach, I'm happy to see a beautifully welcoming and compact space with a double bed on one side of a partition wall and a little seating area with a sink, electric stove, and fridge on the other side leading to a little shower room. Perfect. It's everything I need.

But the sound of the thundering waves is too tempting, and I'm shortly scrambling up and over the grass and gorse covered sand dunes, and what I discover is truly spectacular. For miles and miles in either direction the fine white, sandy beach just seems to go on forever, reaching out to distant mountains further up the coastline. The long curling waves are smoothly rolling in. Before climbing down to the water's edge, I look around me. I'm the only person here in this great expanse of wilderness and feel I've maybe reached the New Zealand I'd imagined.

As I walk barefooted along the silky smooth sand, watching a few coastal birds running and pecking at the shoreline waters, the white crested waves continue to come crashing in, creating the only noise in this magical place.

I wake up from a peaceful night's sleep and before long have pulled on my jeans, and with a just a bit of spitting rain, walk back to the stables. A couple of kids race by on their scramblers while the grazing cattle look up curiously in surprise to watch their antics.

Two horses are tied up outside as I arrive and Rachel, a ginger haired smiling girl, also wanders up with a saddle thrown over her arm.

"Hey you must be Zoë. Let me introduce you to Moon Shine. He's part thoroughbred and should do the job."

I stroke the nose of this beautiful dun horse and he nuzzles me back; glad we've got the formalities over with. Looking up at the sky, Rachel hands me a Swanndri, or to us a fleecy green waterproof anorak, which I tie down securely over the front of the saddle. We mount up, encouragingly make "click, click" sounds to move them forward, and head out down the track.

Again, with things in common, conversation easily flows as I look behind and shout out, "So how come you're here at this place?"

She smiles, kicking her horse to come up alongside mine "I'm earning some holiday money. I'm actually from Alexandra in the South Island but training as a vet at Massey University in

Palmerston North. Believe it or not, it's the only university in New Zealand teaching veterinary practice! I've been at university here for two years, but it's so expensive to travel between the islands that even my mother hasn't visited me yet! Are you ready?"

And with that, we tighten our reins and go galloping along the endless flat white beach. With the power of this animal underneath me and the wind blowing over my face, I'm feeling totally liberated. It's just a feeling too hard to explain when you're at one with the animal and nature's forces. We return to a walk and splash through the waves side by side, feeling this is almost perfect and reminding me, yet again, why I've come to New Zealand.

Rachel asks the same question back, "And you've also come a long way. So why are you here?"

"I've come to find Paradise! This country is so beautiful and diverse, I've already experienced so many things, and it's like heaven here. But on the South Island, I've heard of a hidden and extremely remote place called Paradise, lost in the middle of nowhere. My mission is to go and find it. People say it's the most beautiful place in the world. There's so little information, and what I have found is that, due to its isolation and extreme conditions through mountains and across rivers, there's no way I could reach it by bike. So I've decided to travel to Glenorchy, which is the closest settlement, and use that place as a base to then try and find a way to get to Paradise. Maybe someone can take me or I can get some form of other transport."

Rachel ruminates on what I've just said, "I know you're going to think this is crazy, but coincidentally, I've another vet friend who's working out at the Glenorchy Stables, and maybe they might just do an expedition out to that place. I'll see if I can speak to her and get you contacts."

Continuing on we pass beautiful blue bottle jelly fish that have unfortunately been washed up, and sadly, I also see a small dead black bird.

We both get off our horses, and Rachel carefully kneels down to take a look with her expert eye. "Yes, that's a young albatross that must have gone off course over the ocean and died of exhaustion. You don't see that often, but just sometimes. It must have travelled a long way."

After a few hours we turn back, and immediately the horses start pulling their heads, impatiently trotting back, knowing they're heading home.

Tim walks over carrying cups of coffee and freshly made food and sits down opposite me under the awning of his little café.

"So howz it going? You get a good night's sleep?"

"Yea, that *back* is beautiful, so peaceful and the whole place looks so unspoilt."

He chokes swallowing his coffee and laughs, "No, no it's pronounced '*batch*'! These modest holiday homes are more commonly found in the North Island. In the southern half of the South Island these cabins are mostly in the hills and are called cribs. They're always very, very simple getaway places and mainly near our beaches."

I pick up and devour one of his lovely home baked goat cheese and veggie pies. But it seems bizarre eating pies in the sub-tropics!

And he continues, "A lot of New Zealanders who can't afford a bach will have a permanent camping site in a camping ground for a caravan that will be decorated with seashells, buoys, and fairy lights. I guess like in Europe there's a sub-culture of people who prefer camping. It's a fun community here. People meet up yearly to party with their 'annual holiday mate'. If you get a chance while you're here try and dig out and watch the iconic New Zealand movie *Savage Honeymoon* all about camping, sex, and bikes!"

He takes a sip, and his smile disappears. "But here in the countryside what you see around you is not always paradise. I say it's the kiwi fruit and dairy farmers who are a lot to blame. Some beaches are un-swimmable due to the rivers' 'run off' into these small bays. It's all the intensive dairy farm manure, fertilizers, and animal waste. The sheep industry is also in crisis. We used to have about seventy million sheep, now with their drop in worth, we have maybe now just twenty million. We've got a problem. And you'll hear about this stuff on your travels all over the country."

This guy's a wealth of information, and I can't help but remember something that he might just enlighten me on. "I briefly met a Maori traveller when I was leaving London, and he said something about the Number 8! What's that all about?"

Again he chuckles, "You've probably already seen miles of it. It's fencing wire 0.16" in diameter, used everywhere and iconic. It can be used as a hinge for a stable door, it conducts well as an aerial on a car, and if you get stuck in a ditch people will take out the Number 8 from their car and tow you out with it from their towbar!"

Out of the back of the kitchen a young guy wearing shorts and jandals approaches us carrying more cups of coffee, and Tim turns round to introduce us: "Meet my son Louis."

I reach out to shake his hand. "Hi. So do you also live here?"

He smiles and shakes his head, "Nah, just on holiday. I'm just another Jafa!"

I give him a quizzical look.

He laughs out loud, "Just Another Flippin' Aucklander! And I'm quite happy living in New Zealand. It's a good life."

We spend the next hour cheerfully putting the world to rights, and I'm promised Tim will come and collect me and the bags when I need to leave the bach tomorrow. I drink up my coffee, pay, and tip Louis, who smiles, "Chur Bro!"

Later on, hearing the constant sound of the sea, I wander back down to the wild beach and feel at total peace in what feels like the furthest, most remote place possible. But little do I realise what I'm about to encounter even further north in the Land of the Spirits.

7

LAND OF THE SPIRITS

WAITANGI—RUSSELL
NINETY MILE BEACH—CAPE REINGA

With my defeatist attitude, when leaving I invited Tim to ride my bike back along the sandy road, with me driving his jeep. It didn't stop there. Strangely this morning, I also had a lack of navigational skills to simply land on the doorstop of legend Graeme Crosby, one of New Zealand's greatest racers, who I was told I just had to see and who lived "just spitting distance down the road" in the neighbouring Omaha Valley. It wasn't through lack of perseverance, but I seemed thwarted at every anonymous little intersection and each time took the wrong turn. So I gave up, and after filling up at Wellsford and pulling on my waterproofs due to spitting rain, I was ready to once again attack New Zealand's spine, Highway 1.

Passing giant dairy outfits, the persistent and impatient cars and campers were soon biting my tail. I couldn't continually race ahead to get out of their way, so I was getting used to just pulling over and letting them pass, but with increasing numbers of the massive loggers out in front, road works, and restrictions it was frustratingly slow. I would just wait for the roads to open up every now and again to a dual carriageway to twist that throttle and overtake.

Thankfully, I was soon flying past Whangarei and veered off into a quiet rural undulating stretch of road. This would lead me to Paihia, the pretty little beach town that faced out to the Bay of Islands, opposite Russell and across the bridge from the Waitangi Treaty Grounds.

SeaBed was a grown up kind of luxury backpackers' hostel, more like a chic white stilted home you'd see on Malibu Beach, with my own tastefully decorated room overlooking the beach with its clear blue waters. Besides hearing giggling Germans and laughing American backpackers, I could have been in someone's home. And that's something I really appreciate here in New Zealand; really good places for travellers on restricted budgets.

I stroll over the bridge to the historical and symbolic Waitangi Treaty Grounds, where in 1840 Queen Victoria's representative, William Hobson, and nearly fifty Maori chiefs signed the Treaty of Waitangi. Maori fears were aroused from the start as the settler population grew and demand for land increased, gradually stripping the Maori of control over their affairs. No major concessions were made until 1973, and then February 6 became Waitangi Day and a national holiday. Campaigns and protests continued when, in 1985, Paul Reeves became New Zealand's first Maori Governor General.

The grounds are spectacular, with their sweeping lawns and the Treaty House looking out to the Bay. Intricately carved from three giant kauri trees and protected under a wooden shelter is the eye-watering, largest ceremonial war canoe, or waka taua, in the world. It measures almost thirty-eight metres, which is room enough for eighty paddlers! The richly carved Maori Meeting House was already hosting Maori performers, who were well into their celebrated hake dance when I arrived, sticking their tongues out at me, stamping their feet, and rhythmically shouting in accompaniment. I'd seen this impressive dance only a few times before when watching the New Zealand All Blacks rugby team play in Europe to frighten their opponents.

The very next day I'm following a line of backpack-laden tourists, who look more like a troupe of penguins with their jandals and regimented travel attire, marching to the little "Waimarie" Happy Ferry. Walking into the cabin, I start a friendly banter with the skipper, Ed. He's a happy guy who's in semi-retirement and works just two days a week transporting sixty-two people each time over to isolated Russell on its narrow peninsula, which looks more like an island. After a bit, he laughs and walks away from the helm, leaving me to navigate part of the way over, which for their peace of mind, I'm glad the other travellers didn't see!

I salute the skipper and jump off, zig-zagging between four skiff boats pulled up onto the beach to reach the shoreline of this historic little hillside settlement. This place is full of intrigue and history as I enter the Duke of Marlborough Hotel, famous for holding New Zealand's first liquor licence that they proudly state has been refreshing rascals and reprobates since 1827. Back in the time, Russell, or Kororareka, was a swashbuckling town of whalers and sealers with a reputation as the "Hellhole of the Pacific," with forty bars and twenty brothels. But the legend goes even further back. It's told that a Maori chief, wounded in battle, asked for a penguin broth, and this is how the place got its name. After drinking it he said, "ka reka te korora"; *korora* (the blue penguin) and *reka* (sweet), translating to "how sweet is the penguin."

Sitting looking out over the tree-lined terrace and out to the bay, I curiously pick up and glance at the *Marlborough Mail Newsletter*. It starts with the headline "No relief in sight for muggy night with a month of sticky nights to come! Sub-tropical air and warm seas are leading to unbearable, sleepless nights and it's going to be around for the next month. Across the country main centres have been sweltering with temperatures warmer than average." So I guess I'm hopefully not going to be pulling on those extra layers for a while yet.

It's also true to say the majority of New Zealanders are now back to work or getting ready for it after the long holidays. Now, with what looks like just the tourists, it sadly feels a little bit like Disney put his stamp on the place, as no locals can be heard and all the hospitality staff seem to be other nationals, either on exchange placements, sabbaticals, or earning money for further backpacking trips.

But walking back to the jetty, I notice a discreet hidden flight of stairs leading to the curious and exotic sounding "Bay of Islands Swordfish Club". It's just twenty steps away from the shouting crowds as I enter a silent, empty clubhouse filled with historic trophies and boards listing the champion anglers and their massive record weight catches, from blue marlin, hammerheads, to yellow tails. Giant record-breaking fish are suspended from the walls of this colonial looking place. I look up at one plaque carved as a massive fish with the carved words "This 1017lb Blue Marlin caught in the Bay of Islands in 1967 was flown to the United States the same month to publicize New Zealand at the Los Angeles Sportsmen's Vacation and Travel Show where it was much the biggest exhibit!"

It certainly feels like an adventuress place as I jump off the boat back in Pahia, wander into Charlotte's Kitchen, and grab a sofa on the deck looking out to the string of little islands. And apparently it wasn't just men who were famous here for their exploits. It goes that Charlotte Badger, this eatery's namesake, was defiant and said to be an immoral woman who used her feminine energies to incite the mutiny of a crew and took over the ship *Venus*. She joined the fray with pistol and sword and headed to the Bay of Islands, having also masterminded the pirating of yet another ship. When she arrived, her fate is not clear, other than it's believed she became friendly with a Maori chief!

This is definitely a place for sailing, and having passed my competent crew course a few years previously, I just need to pin down a boat to get back out onto. So the following day walking along the seafront and past a Maori fisherman preparing a massive kingfish head as today's bait, I approach a sixty-five foot ocean sailing yacht. It had been chartered for the day to take out a handful of people to get closer to some of the islands, swim out around them, and maybe find the odd dolphins or penguins along the way.

But disaster literally strikes me before we've even raised the anchor! Climbing up and over onto the deck, I slip and crash my bespectacled eyes and forehead into the metal rail of the low cabin entrance. The severe hit creates absolute agony, and blood is dripping everywhere. I automatically go into shock mode. My left thumb and index fingers are uncontrollably trembling, and I'm feeling my veins and muscles between them palpitating, twitching, and thumping. One of the crew leads me into the cabin, and I'm given tissues to hold down onto the deep cut. I have no mirror so don't see the gravity of it all but am adamant, at least in my mind, that I'll carry on for the day, reassuring everyone I'm just fine. Which I'm not! The head's thumping as I pull my baseball cap down and my dark glasses on my ever darkening eye to avoid any further questions.

Finally sitting out on the deck, the day passes sublimely as we sail over to Waewaetorea Island and anchor on the south side for a little swim over to its shore. We follow a fleet of racing super yachts on the way back and then are spontaneously joined by a playful school of dolphins riding our boat's waves to also race us!

Climbing out of the boat, the skipper worryingly looks at me stating, "Go see a doctor, or at least a chemist, as I'm not happy. I can see a blood spot on the white of your eye."

So without further ado, I find myself facing a white coated pharmacist looking into my eye. "What do you see? Are you dizzy? There's blood on the eye. You should really call a doctor if it spreads. But it's not on the iris, which is good. I'm putting a big plaster over the cut to keep it together to avoid having stitches. After a few days, take these Steri-Strips, lay them crossways over the scar on the eyebrow, leave for a week, and then replace again."

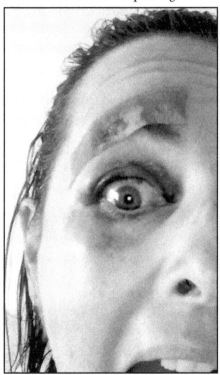

I peer nervously into the mirror back at the hostel and am greeted by a massive black eye with blue and purple bruising all around and spreading down to my cheekbone. I look like I've been punched in the face. My hands are still trembling, which lasts well into the night, and I'm just glad I'm not leaving today. Boy, do I look sexy! But I smile, as I can at least see and ironically know it wasn't an accident caused while riding the bike!

The next morning, looking reluctantly again into the mirror at my battered purple, pink, and yellow swollen right eye, I lightheartedly select a lovely matching mauve eye shadow for the left eye, and with a bit of concealer dabbed onto the cheek, hey presto, it doesn't appear so dramatic.

Pulling out of Paihia, I automatically stop at the first gas station to fill up and notice a Dutch guy with a Honda 650cc at the next pump doing the same thing. He smiles but doesn't hide the fact that he's jealous learning I've still a long way to go. Although he's leaving tomorrow and covered an incredible 6,000 kilometres in just three weeks, he's claiming he could do it all over again! Waving back to each other, we head off in opposite directions, and with just a meagre 167 kilometres to cover today, it's not long before I'm in Northland sailing through the wonderful Twin Coast Discovery Highway 10. I meander through the beautiful green sloping lands and river crossings and hit great straight roads where I cheekily can't help but exceed the 100km/hr limits!

But it's on a small hillside, outside a farmhouse, that I come to a stop to look out at the delicious views, but not for the reason most people would. From a long driveway a truck approaches, and a Maori with his wife leans out of the window, "Good day. Can we help?"

"Hope you don't mind, but I'm just taking some snaps of your beautiful Number 8 spanning the horizon!"

They giggle, "Yea for sure. Go ahead; it's all yours!" and drive off waving.

Crossing the pretty little Kaeo River and hearing the loud noise of crickets, I come to another halt to breathe in the atmosphere. A trucker approaches from the opposite direction and brakes sharply kindly asking, "Hey, I saw you standing by the bike. Have you got any problems? Do you need a ride back into town?"

I smile, putting my thumbs up that all's good, but deep down appreciate the unsolicited offer of help. And the only other place I stop off at is just past Doubtless Bay, close to Taipa. It's purely due to curiosity, as it's a place with my maiden name, the Matthews Farm and Vintage Collection. The cheery Winston Matthews literally welcomes me like a long lost relative! He's a third generation of farmers originally coming over from Oxfordshire in the 1830s. His collection of tractors dating back to the 1920s is amazing, which I smile about due to my father previously being a Massey Ferguson dealer back in Herefordshire. But it's not just tractors he collects, as there are an eclectic range of fire engines, horse carriages, bikes, radios, nickers made out of flour bags, stuffed birds, and a famous "Trekka," which was the only vehicle ever manufactured in New Zealand, back in the '60s, and looking very similar to the Land Rover.

Then for the first time today, I turn west, leaving Highway 1 and ride through smaller, narrower roads to the settlement of Kaitaia. But that's not before stopping at a local farmers market to stock up on fresh New Zealand produce, as again, and not for the first time, where I'm going may be pretty remote and I'll need to be self-sufficient. Then it's another half-hour ride along the straight flat farmland Kaitaia-Awaroa Road and onto a long narrow road hugging the Tasman Sea. Almost literally at the end of the road, it's here I finally pull up at an atmospheric 1880s timber homestead right across from a large wild stretch of beach. Surf boards are leaning, piled up against the walls, as I take my helmet off and walk up and into the dark kauri wood lined hallway. This quiet place is heaven as I drop my bags down on the double bed and look out from my window to the peaceful quiet sea and a swinging hammock down in the garden below.

Astonishingly, this is yet another hostel, with my own room, but feels more like an upmarket B&B. It also feels like I've got the place to myself as I walk barefoot across the sand drifted road to the vast expanse of beach with large tropical tree covered hills on one side and giant sand dunes squeezed in between them. And it's here vans of all sizes are driving onto the flat, hard sands, and motorcycles are unloaded to race across them. Everyone I'm seeing now are Maoris. I jump around in surprise as a sprightly Welsh black and white sheepdog runs from the hostel with a Frisbee, pleading for me to pull it from its mouth and fling it away.

But the real reason for coming all this way is to reach the very northern tip of New Zealand, otherwise known as Cape Reinga, where it's said the spirits of the Maori dead depart from this world. And on the way up there, I also want to witness the spectacular Ninety Mile Beach that runs alongside this narrow peninsula.

With the temperatures having soared to a seasonally high twenty-eight degrees during the day and with warm rain pounding down later in the evening with the sounds of pounding waves, this ticks all the boxes that I'm happily in the sub-tropics.

Through the crack in the curtains, the rising sun wakes me up, and before long, my entire body feels exhilarated to be riding alongside the crashing surf on this quiet stretch of road. About half an hour further up and past Awanui, I see the first sign to access the Ninety Mile Beach, which in reality is sixty-four miles long. The sign leads me for another twelve kilometres through pretty countryside with its farms, cattle, and forests until I literally can't go any further and stop at a sandy covered car park with giant sand dunes hiding the sea. I carefully park the bike on a hard patch of sand, put a piece of cereal cardboard paper under the foot stand, and walk up through the dunes to be amazed at what I see. Again, without exaggerating, there are endless expanses of beach and crashing waves going out into the horizons in either direction. I'm also spoilt as this time early in the day; there's just nobody else around. Back on the bike, my journey continues through increasingly larger expanses of vistas with jaw dropping views from hilltops leading the eye through tropical green, sun-drenched valleys to faraway giant white sand dunes and the sea licking the sky out on the horizon.

Once again, I can go no further and reach Cape Reinga, where I walk up a hilly slope to the edge of land where the Tasman and Pacific Oceans come clashing together creating waves and whirlpools in the middle of this vast expanse of waters. At this meeting point, it's said they represent the coming together of man and woman and the creation of life. The Maori believe that the spirits start their journey by sliding down the roots of an 800-year-old pohutukaura tree into the ocean; they climb out again at Ohaua—the highest of the Three Kings Islands, to bid final farewells before returning to their ancestors in Hawaiki, the legendary homeland of the Polynesians. In this magical place I say a little prayer out to everyone and also for my own safety.

In deep thought, I return to the bike, putting my leather jacket back on, ready to leave. A Maori tour leader walks up to me smiling. "Hey, you're the girl with that Triumph jacket. I must have passed you at least twice in my van. I'm ferrying Americans and Germans. You got it right, leaving here now before all the buses come winding up here later in the morning to visit this place and the lighthouse. You ride safe now."

He's right. I've got a challenging long ride back, and after what will be a fairly strenuous couple of hours, I'm already imagining resting peacefully in that swaying hammock. So I say goodbye to this mystical land, and finally I'm riding the straight country road close to Ahipara. I'm exhausted and already hearing the continuous and repetitive waves crashing alongside me it feels like a dream ...

... Suddenly, out of nowhere on this empty road, an oncoming small truck mysteriously appears with a camper van accelerating to overtake it. The camper can't see me on the other side and narrowly misses knocking me over as I swerve, out of control to keep my balance, onto the grassy verge. I close my eyes to gain composure, but on opening them, I see further down the road a silver rat bike with a rolled-up bag across it's handlebars has screeched to an almost stop, whips up a U-ie, and races back to me. Everything feels like it's in a haze. The face of the rider is covered with a bandana face mask, and besides his dark penetrating brown eyes, I see no other expression. His voice is deep and warmly comforting in searching to know if everything is alright, having witnessed the deathly close encounter from behind the trucks.

And like that, I'm following him towards and past Ahipara, up and around to Shipwreck Bay. We come to a stop, and he pulls his bandana off, exposing the most beautiful, calm face. He leads me down to this lost beach and we're soon intertwined in the dunes, yearning for each other's bodies. The softness of his caresses over my skin is mesmerizing, and slowly I become enveloped in total ecstasy. It's been a long time since I've felt this way . . .

I jolt out of a deep comatose sleep, hearing the radio bizarrely playing ELO's *Strange Magic* and opening my eyes see the collie licking my feet dangling from the hammock. I look around dis-orientated and see the bike parked up and wondering what I've actually done and what was just a dream. But that night I fall asleep with a deep smile.

The very next morning, and back to reality, I just about manage to tear off the bandage over my eye from the boating episode and place the binding tape back over it. I look like some sort of mercenary soldier, and I'm fine with that, as long as people don't think I've been beaten up!

The day's spent lazing on the beach, cooking a whole trevally fish, and watching giant butterflies fluttering up and over me. But the quiet is soon broken later in the afternoon as a large extended Chinese family arrive with their pots, pans, chopsticks, and boxes and boxes of food. The children, needing to stretch their legs, scamper out into the garden towards the beach, but instead rush immediately to the table tennis, where they pick up the racquets and start whacking the ball back and forth over the net. On this public holiday weekend, they later tell me it had been a long five-hour trip for them from Auckland.

So before they start cooking Chinese delights in our shared kitchen, I bring my food outside, throwing the occasional titbit to the little sheepdog. Pink rays flood the pale blue sky as the sun sets. The beach is now empty, and quiet peace is now all there is in this magical place.

8

CALM BEFORE THE STORM

OREWA—MORE PUBLIC HOLIDAYS
RAGLAN—CATAMARAN SAILING

Without a doubt, today was going to be a much longer than expected journey to head back south and reach the outskirts of Auckland. Looking at the road maps, I was already beginning to realize that what I thought might just be a small diversion to go see something interesting would add massive distance and hours onto the already pre-planned 400-kilometre route. Although I had been recommended to bike down to the Waipoua Kauri Forest to touch the huge ancient Tane Mahuta tree this would clock up an extra ninety kilometres each way, with high probability of unpaved, difficult roads that would naturally add to the stress in controlling the heavy bike.

I also knew that by pure coincidence today, 29 January, was the Auckland Anniversary Day. This was yet another public holiday, this time observed by the northern half of the North Island celebrating the arrival of William Hobson, later the first governor of New

Zealand, in the Bay of Islands in 1840. I couldn't have chosen a worse day to travel here, as everyone and their mother would be heading home. As a matter of necessity, I tuned into the local radio station to hear the weather forecast, which unsurprisingly, left me a little shocked: "Auckland and Northland is set for another two days of fine weather hitting the high 20s before the remnants of the tropical cyclone will blanket the country in rain and strong winds. The next few days look great, but on Thursday things will turn nasty as the ex-tropical cyclone moves further in, bringing north-easterly winds, which could develop to gales with heavy rain. Try and enjoy the sun and the heat while you can!"

So the decision's made. With an early start, I'll get back onto Highway 1 to try and cover as much mileage as quickly as possible. I twist the throttle, the engine lets out a roar, and within a blink of an eye, I've left this heavenly quiet, lost place. I'd almost forgotten about those awkward winding roads I'd come up on, through the mountains and over high vistas on this northern stretch of the highway, but riding it in the opposite direction is again totally captivating as I was lead down and approached Whangarei.

But with a click of a finger it all changes. The ever increasing stream of cars and trucks had appeared and were now pushing impatiently to get past me. I am more or less half way, so I decide to stop for a mental break, as well as a food one. Looking out onto the road, scoffing my bacon, avocado, and egg filled bagel, I'm starting to see the beginning of a massive tail-to-tail southbound flow of traffic. My destination for today is Orewa, and although it's only another hundred-odd kilometres and doesn't sound like much, it is going to take quite a while to filter through and overtake all this traffic. I pull away, and even here, the stop-start backup is seriously beginning. So with total determination, on this hot morning with temperatures soaring to record highs, I pull my sun visor down and for the next couple of hours am forced to stop, start, pull out, ride, and filter between traffic coming heavily from both directions. My sweaty, gloved hands are stuck tightly to the handlebars, which I know is wrong, but I'm nervous and feeling uncomfortable, as extreme concentration is now needed to avoid even the slightest of mishaps. I don't think anyone would call this fun.

Already fifty kilometres out of Auckland, the traffic has come to an almost grid lock. I'm just pleased to be staying this side of the city tonight! Stopping at the next gas station to fill up, this time two cheerful New Zealand bikers come walking over to me for the habitual chat about where we're all going and warning that our lives are sometimes in the hands of these crazy, bad drivers and to be extra careful! I just hope my spirit friends are with me to protect me.

Five and a half hours later from the time I'd set off, I ride into the Orewa Pillows Backpackers Motel. Sighing deeply with relief, I pull out the ignition key and walk over to the reception office. A Chinese guy in a string vest, picking his teeth with a toothpick, murmurs something, and handing me a key, leads me through a sad looking, overgrown grass courtyard with dirty, grubby plastic chairs and nine bedroom doors facing into it. Even the pigeons look dejected. They don't even try to fly away when I walk past. He points to a kitchen area and a laundry room next to what look like uni-sex toilets and showers. Next to that a bedroom door is wide open, with a woman lying on a bed looking like she's smoking a joint while a couple of slippered Chinese men shuffle past me shouting so loudly that I feel I'm somewhere in a rural Chinese market place. Two doors down, I enter my simple room and dump my bags. Bizarrely, in this strange place the bed has immaculate, perfectly ironed white sheets. The Chinese owners must be in the laundry business!

It's time to stretch these legs and take a look around Orewa. But I quickly notice this is a place of extremes. Walking out from the

Motel across the Hibiscus Coast Highway, I feel like I'm entering another world, as large luxury beachfront apartment blocks lead me onto an immaculately kept conifer-lined beach walkway overlooking the receding sea. This is another beautiful place with the surf-paragliders skimming and jumping off the waves, kids running and screaming into the sea with their surfboards, and distant yachts tacking and gybing along the coastline. But there's no denying the fact that it's a busier than normal day here, with sun worshippers spread out on blankets under the trees and families eating from generous laden picnic baskets. And I also feel great to be part of the festive holiday mood, and all I need do now is slap on some more suntan cream and relax to the sound of the sea. By the end of the afternoon the waves have come back in and have totally covered the beach and are once more lapping up onto the shoreline rocks. It's a signal to return to "the other side of the tracks," cook up some food that will probably be the pasta I'd stuffed in my bag, drink some wine, and plan the route for tomorrow.

Walking into the kitchen, I start looking through the cupboards to see what I can cook my food with. They're all nearly empty, with no glasses or cutlery. At the same time, a blonde-haired hippie Aussie girl is taking something from the fridge. I smile, "Are there are any wine glasses?"

She smiles and simply says, "Nah, they've all been stolen!"

That's nice! At the same moment a giant, and that's not exaggerating, tattooed guy comes ambling in carrying a case full of empty beer bottles, which he duly dumps on the floor and in exchange carries back out a full box. I quickly grab a mug, filling it with wine, then walk out to the courtyard, picking up a fallen plastic chair to sit on. I discreetly look around and notice the woman who'd been lying on her bed is waddling out now dressed in jeans and a grubby shirt, with the glummest of faces, towards the shower block. Sitting close by is a smiling "red smudged, over- lipsticked" woman with her husband from Mangakino. I smile, noticing they're also sipping their wine from two white mugs.

They pull their chairs closer to me. I smile and raise my mug. "Cheers!"

They laugh, "Yes, no glasses here!"

But the old man is looking at me cautiously then asks directly, "Can I ask? How did you get that black eye?"

I teasingly reply, "Do you want to know the truth?"

Their eyes widen in anticipation. "Yes!"

"Nothing bad. It was during sailing the other day!"

They look back almost with a sigh of relief.

Needing to get my pasta cooked, I walk back to the kitchen, and the same, but this time burping, tattooed guy walks in and cracks open yet another bottle of beer. While I'm watching over the boiling saucepan, a few minutes later he's walked back again to repeat the exercise with another bottle. I watch him leave to join another inebriated Chinese guy sitting out at the front under the porch. By the time I'm piling the pasta onto my plate, this time it's the Chinese guy who's walked in to explode open another beer. I walk out to the garden, and this repetitive show continues as I scoop up the pasta with a plastic spoon I'd found deep in my tank bag. Then another bigger than average guy wanders over and past me, coughing like his lungs are going to explode. The other two guys continually rush past me to relieve themselves in the toilets, as by now they've obviously drunk too much. Then to top it all off, a drunk Korean carpenter from Christchurch (I know this because he shouted this to me) wants to talk about everything and nothing with me. I've had enough, and I think I'll be double-locking my room tonight.

I quickly eat up, and as I'm about to leave, another Korean man walks, in more of a straight line than the others, towards me. He's perhaps noticed the other guys parading up and down past me and in stilted English blurts out, "Now listen. If someone causes a problem, I'm upstairs. Just call me. Me, I'm on a building project here. I'm a Taekwondo expert. Nobody mucks around with me. I'm younger than you. You my step mother. I look after you."

With that last farcical performance, I'm done for the day, rush into my room, lock myself in, draw the curtains together from any prying eyes, and turn the TV on that, unsurprisingly, only offers Chinese speaking channels.

The next morning, after a happily uninterrupted night, I switch the radio on to hear that there's now a constant threat as temperatures are soaring across the country. Emergency measures are being taken. Pets and children are being taken out of hot locked cars and people are being told to keep cool in this warmer than normal weather that's been hitting almost thirty degrees.

With over 200 kilometres to cover before I reach the laid-back surfing and artists' community of Raglan, I make a small diversion and bike down to the Coffee Club on the main strip to start the day with a plate full of bacon and eggs washed down with a mug of coffee. Fully replenished and putting my jacket back on next to the bike, a female bus driver unexpectedly passes me, kindly smiles, and sticks her thumb up in approval. I smile back, and with just that tiny bit of reciprocal positivity that makes it a good start to the day.

As soon as I'm back on the highway and with ever darkening clouds starting to blow in, I immediately start to see speed restriction signs, with the holiday traffic starting to once again build up out in front. There are no visible road works here yet, but the authorities must have already spent a fortune on these millions of orange road cones that are everywhere bordering the miles and miles of roads. This is a sure indication that there's going to be massive work undertaken for the future expansion of the country's roads. Somehow I feel the place will never be quite the same again.

It feels like the entire Auckland area is grid-locked with all lanes at a standstill. I've never seen anything quite like this so far out from a city. Once again, like a déjà vu experience, I have no other choice but for the next hour to filter through lanes of impatient traffic. This major city really could be anywhere in the world facing the same day to day problems of congestion and commuter stress.

Finally leaving the urban sprawl behind, the sun comes out in celebration, the road has narrowed to just one lane, and there's minimal traffic. The ride is a breeze passing through flat grasslands and meadows until I reach the emerald-green Waikato River where Hamilton, New Zealand's fourth largest city, stands. Signs tell me it's time to turn off onto Highway 23, and keeping a careful eye on the map, I ride due west, winding up and down through the hilly terrain until I reach the outskirts of Raglan. I check the address again and curse seeing I've gone too far, so turn round and climb back up a hilly road that looks out over Lorenzen Bay and westwards to Whaingaroa Harbour. I descend down a gritty driveway surrounded in tropical vegetation, finally leading down to a hidden house overlooking the bay. This is a place in quite a spectacular location and for all the right reasons.

Rick, the host and well known artist with a gallery and studio in the arty area of Raglan Wharf, welcomes me to his beautiful home, which is precariously balanced on the cliff-side. Without exaggeration my room is a dream, with three external glass walls looking far out to the beautiful estuary. All I can see is sky, tropical vegetation, and water.

From my gleeful look, Rick's eyes light up, and he smiles back, "Yea, it's quite a place here isn't it? If you climb the couple of hundred steep steps down this cliff, I've got a tiny beach and mooring where I keep my forty-foot catamaran. If you like sailing, and before the predicted storm comes in tomorrow, we could get out tonight. And I know we're a bit out of town, but it's slow at the studio at the moment so I'm happy to show you around a bit."

And true to his word, a little later on he drops me off in town to take a wander and says he'll be back shortly to drive me round the coast. This is a wonderful place, and I can understand why a lot of people often stay far longer than they intended. It has an incredibly laid-back feel as I walk along palm shaded roads with hip cafés and pubs, bohemian arts and crafts shops, and surfing stores. It has a real edge. But the main lure is for the surfing community, as the waters here feature some of the best left-handed breaks in the world, and Rick had promised we'd go and visit some of those famous bays and beaches.

Before long, I'm seated with Rick at the cool Shack Café eating a delicious late lunch. "I've closed the gallery and thought we'd do a circular little drive around the coastline and back inland to show you some of the highlights we have here. It's true that there are great waves all around the country, but Raglan has to be one of New Zealand's finest surfing destinations. All you can see around here are lines of perfect breakers. The best place for inexperienced surfers is Ngarunai Beach, just five kilometres away. But for the experienced and pros, the main breaks are found at Whale Bay and Manu Bay. You ready?"

I sure am and jump into Rick's van as he drives us out of town to first look out at Whale Bay, where the horizontally jointed rocks lay bare far out to sea from the receding tide.

He looks out to the horizon. "This is funny. The one day you come to see this place to watch the surfers, there's no waves, and they haven't bothered to turn up. The sea is as flat as a pancake!"

We continue onto Manu Bay, which is also void of surfers. It's here we start driving up steep dirt tracks and up along grassy hills, high up from the sea, where contented cows are looking over the Number 8 and out to the turquoise blue sea and the cloudless azure sky, making it difficult to distinguish where one starts and the other finishes. Following the track, we stop at the Mt. Karioi lookout, where the spectacular giant green-grassed mountain slopes drop dramatically down into the sea far, far below us, with the clear vista showing us the perfect left-handed breakers crashing against the cliffs.

Slowly descending, we reach Ruapuke Beach for a walk along the warm soft sand. The black beach is famed for its silver and bronze sparkling speckles of sand that glint in the sunshine. Tiny baby mussels are attached to and cover the beach rocks, making even these also appear black. Rick has one last surprise as we head back and stop to walk down the steep pathway to Bridal Veil Falls, hidden away in dense native bush. White water plummets fifty-five metres down a sheer rock face into a green pool, and we have the place all to ourselves. But I wasn't quite prepared for the rigorous walk back up that took us almost half an hour.

Much later in the afternoon, sitting out on the terrace, all I can hear are the noisy cicada up in the trees, who've been making one hell of a noise during the day and are synonymous here with the summer. Often colloquially called locusts, they're not the true ones, and once dark comes, like turning a light switch off, their screeching stops. And all this noise stops totally in the winter. Rick casually walks over. "If you're still up for it, we could take the catamaran out tonight for the sunset. I'm sorry to say it's only forecast for three to four knots of wind, so we may need to use the engine, but this place is magical out on the water at night, plus some of my other sailing buddies might be out too. I need to go back and lock the studio up, so see you later."

And with that he's gone. An hour before the sun sets and with the tide fully in, Rick and I climb down the steep cliff's steps, wade into the water, heaving ourselves up onto the catamaran, untie the buoys, and pull the anchor up. We sail out in the quiet, empty waters with the golden sun slowly sinking making the tropical sky turn a deep orange and red. Life feels good as I drink a glass of chilled white wine while decadently lying on the trampoline netting. Shortly after, Rick miraculously produces a fresh salmon linguine that he'd just magically cooked up before leaving and brought onto the boat in insulated containers to keep warm! These are some of the moments to savour and try to never forget.

The next morning, I once again look into my eye, and this time the blood spot has thankfully disappeared. I finally peel the plaster off above my brow, but on the down-side, my face is still bruised, which I stoically try to hide with a bit of concealer. Left to my own devices, I sunbathe on the sloping boarded terrace, which feels to be only precariously balanced on wooden stilts and feeling like they're going to give way at any moment. It's now I have time to reflect. I'm feeling contented. I've turned a chocolate mocha brown from the country's sweltering heatwave of a summer and have stopped wearing makeup, feeling I don't need to prove anything to the outside world. It's taken time to peel off those layers of urban life and subconscious social commitments we feel we need to adhere to in order to make ourselves feel or look more attractive.

By mid-afternoon the clock's ticking by in finding out when the storm is going to arrive. The clouds have ominously swept in, covering the skies, and the winds are becoming increasingly stronger and more violent, mercilessly knocking and bashing the palms and cabbage trees around like toy puppets.

Rick looks outside. "All this weather may also be something to do with the show appearing later tonight; a 'super moon eclipse'—a blue moon and a total lunar eclipse is simultaneously happening. If we can see through the clouds, it's going to be a rare glimpse of something that hasn't appeared in 150 years."

But later in the evening, we're forced to close the windows from the winds. I have a massively demanding journey tomorrow, and I'm just praying the main storm will have kept away and everything here will have calmed down.

9

STUCK ON THE FORGOTTEN HIGHWAY

CYCLONE FEHI—MUD, MUD, MUD—RESCUE PLAN

During the night I'm jolted awake several times by the thunder and pounding rain, which worries me that the storm could continue to worsen. Just before dawn, or about 5:30, the trees along the shore are still being battered. My resilient or maybe stupid self tells me I have no choice, and an hour later I'm up with the howling winds. And shortly after, I've left a goodbye and thank you note for Rick and hauled my bag back out and tied it onto the bike. Incredibly, it's not raining, which I can't quite believe, so I don't bother to put on my waterproof trousers.

I pat the tank, saying we'll be alright, and pushing against the wind arrive at the Raglan petrol station. I look down at my watch. It's 7:30AM, and although I know the route will cover about 300 kilometres, I've no idea how long it will take with the current conditions. The plan is to head south and enter SH43, a rugged and desolate 149-kilometre road that twists through the hills west of Taumarunui. But worryingly, out on that road I'd been warned and made aware of a twelve-kilometre stretch somewhere through the Tangarakau Gorge which is totally unsealed. And I still haven't quite worked out whether it's before or after my final destination tonight at Whangamomona. With the massive 250 kilos of metal and bags I've no idea how I'll cope in manoeuvring it.

On this cold, cloud-covered misty morning, I ride leisurely up to the large urban sprawl of Hamilton and just outside hit Highway 3, which leads me through valleys densely populated with silently grazing dairy herds. This rural landscape south of Hamilton is known as the "King Country" because it was the refuge of King Tawhiao after he and his clan were driven south during the New Zealand wars. The area soon gained a reputation among Pakeha, or the white New Zealanders, as a Maori stronghold, unwelcoming and renowned for difficult terrain that meant few, if any, Europeans, dared enter. Sadly, the forest's safety was short-lived when peace was declared in 1881, and the loggers descended in droves.

Continuing south, I pass the dairy farming town of Otorohanga, which also celebrates anything to do with kiwis. Signs, statues, and pictures of the birds are everywhere. But it's riding up through Hangatiki that I stop at the Kiwi House and Sanctuary, which was the first place in the world where the public could view a kiwi in captivity. The place is empty of any activity, as I conclude it's still too early, so I turn back. But it's now beginning to spit with that habitual four letter word—*rain*! I pull up behind a gas station with the trucks and pull on my waterproof trousers.

Both roads, Highway 3 and now Highway 4, are long, long and longer than shown on the map, and the views out onto the horizon are becoming increasingly dark and uninviting. It seems to be getting miserably colder, and it's already feeling for me like a tough slog without much respite or enjoyment. But thankfully at this stage, I had no idea what I would be challenged with further on! Almost four and a half hours into the ride, I enter the small township of Taumarunui, the entrance point up into Highway 43, or better known as the "Forgotten World Highway," to fill the tank to bursting point, knowing there'd be nothing up on that remote road.

I tightly zip up my jacket, pull my fleece neck warmer further up and over my chin, pull my gloves back on, and kick the shift pedal down. The start is good as I enter a well-tarmacked road that leads me up and through gentle undulating land, but which increasingly becomes surrounded by larger and larger mist-covered hills and mountains. This remote place looks like it's been thrashed by the storm, with the surfaces drenched and streams of water running down the steep sides of the road into the water table drainage systems on either side. But, at least for the moment, it's not raining.

Maybe due to the weather, there's little or no traffic as I sojourn on through this increasingly dense, tropical vegetation, and the only thing I notice passing me is a sign telling me it's forty-fine kilometres to my destination at Whangamomona.

And then I see it! The asphalt covered road has stopped, and replacing it up ahead as far as the eye can see and disappearing round an inclining corner, is a mud laden, water soaked, stony, rubble-covered track. My living nightmare! This must be the twelve-kilometre stretch of unpaved road that everyone had talked about. I have no other option. I breathe deeply and slowly ride the bike onto it. But I can already feel the problem. There's no traction. Just the day before this was a dry, dusty road that was relatively easy to ride. But the storm had come in last night and flooded the road, turning it into a deep, slushy mud bath.

I start to ride with extra caution, but I'm scarily slipping and sliding on this heavy bike, which while on this lonely road terrifies me, as I know I won't be able to pick it up. I immediately stop and breathe in deeply to again gain my composure. There's no other option but to find a way to continue. Knowing they'll never be totally flat on the ground, I gently put my feet down as far as possible on either side of the bike to maintain some form of stability, only to find they're sinking into inches of mud.

I start to rev the bike back into life and slowly "walk it" through, which for me and what I'm riding, is impossible terrain. But on numerous occasions, with the balancing act of gently accelerating and moving it forward in the mud, it helplessly stalls. I just hope to God I don't flood the engine with my repeated efforts to re-ignite the bike. I continue and then scarily see the start of steep cambers sloping down around the corners into water-filled gullies that could so easily take and slide the bike into them. Above all else, I need to try and keep the bike upright in the centre of the road, irrespective if any traffic that approaches or passes me. I have to be the priority!

Paddle-walking the heavy bike, I'm feeling totally useless and petrified as I navigate around an ever increasing number of fallen trees and branches obstructing my passage along the road. It's almost impossible to manoeuvre around the sloping, tight corners. I stop again for breath from this purely physical task. After about an hour of hell, I feel like screaming, crying, and giving up. The bike's almost slipped over three times and only been saved by some magic strength I didn't even know I had. Getting trapped under the bike, sinking into the mud, and unable to lift it up is unthinkable.

It's then I hear three cars coming towards me from behind, and at a snail's pace, they carefully manoeuvre around me. Two pass on the right and the third on the left. And then it happens. The third car loses total grip, slides, and falls over sideways into the deep water table ditch. I look in horror, but there's nothing I can do, as I'm also struggling just to keep the bike up from falling over in the same way.

I've lost track of time. A set of three cruel teasers comes my way when the slimy mud changes to asphalt over three bridges but wickedly changes back. Riding over this third bridge, a couple in a white car pass and wave over to me with some kind of sign language but just keep driving on. I wonder why. I'm in need of some sort of help. I've no idea how far away the settlement is where I'm headed, as the battery in my phone has finally decided to die, and so I can't even make contact for help. After a while, with the mud that's got up to my ankles and totally drowned my boots, I come to the end of this muddy hell. The little white car with the kind New Zealand couple has been waiting patiently there all the time to make sure I got through. I smile, with a lump in my throat and almost in tears, with the deepest gratitude. And it's here ironically that the rain starts to pour down. But within a few miles, I ride round a bend and see the warmest welcome from the Whangamomona Hotel, the remotest pub in New Zealand and headquarters of the Republic.

I come to a stop in front of this wooden-stilted colonial white building and, without thinking, simply rush with my helmet still on inside to the bar with its warm, log burning fireplace. Trembling from the cold, I spurt out, "Brrrrr! Give me a drink! Whatever! I don't care!"

The young guy polishing glasses behind the bar smiles and hands me a beer with a whiskey shot on the side, which I down in one. The spirit hits and burns the back of my throat, but the warmth calms me. I can't quite believe it's taken me seven hours since I left this morning. Without a doubt, this is the worst day's ride of the trip, if not my worst ever! I'm soaked, so after a warm shower and laying all my wet clothes, sodden books and maps out on the radiators, chairs, and anywhere "hangable" in my little room, I wander back down to absorb and get to know this bizarre but life-saving place.

A group of casually dressed guys are seated around the bar drinking beers and discussing stuff, which I later learn is the town's board meeting!

One of the guys in shorts and black wellie boots turns around to raise his glass to me, "Are you the girl on that bike outside? How the hell did you get here?"

I smile, "I guess with a lot of luck. There's a car still back there that slid over and couldn't get up! It's dangerous up there."

"Well I never! Hi, I'm Tony, and that's my brother, John Herlihy, the Republic's fifth human President of Whangamomona. There have also been a goat and a dog with the distinguished title! You may not know, but thirty years ago this tiny town, originally in the Taranaki region, revolted in protest to the government's decision to include us in the Whanganui/Manawatu region, and so we broke away from New Zealand, forming our own republic! Yea, I'm a trucker for my sins, and I know this road real well. It's a good thing you didn't come earlier. The logging trucks go through at 6AM!"

I swallow hard, envisaging the horror and potential disaster had I met one of those giants who would not have stopped in time on that slippery track!

"Yea, I also drilled seven years ago the coal seam for gas with seven well sites in that area, and back then the gorge route was empty. Now there's a lot more traffic. Let's get you something to eat. Here's the menu. The fish and chips are good."

After killing off my hunger pangs, John also ambles over in what I'm starting to see are the obligatory black gum boots and sits down next to me. "So do you want to get your passport stamped while you're here so you're legal?" and smiling, "in return for having a sit on your bike!"

I eagerly nod, pulling the passport out of my bag, "Thank you. So how is the Republic?"

He mulls the question over, "Well I'm actually a sheep farmer, and only sixteen people currently live in the town. But we're happy to be independent since 1989, after the government altered the provincial boundaries solely on watersheds, removing us from the district of Taranaki, saying Whanga's waters ended up in the sea at Whanganui. We were obviously grumpy about this, not wanting the bureaucrats in Palmerston North telling us what to do. So a revolt mushroomed, and ways and means were sought to protest against this evil tyranny.

"But I like your royals. The queen is probably outdated herself, but the young ones are pretty popular and still have plenty to offer. There's been a lot in the papers recently about Meghan and Harry and their upcoming wedding. When Harry came last time it was $40,000 a day, but he's as popular as hell and there was no question of the government not paying. Last time, he didn't even call in, the mongrel, he should've called in and had a beer or a cup of tea."

I smile back, "Everyone is so welcoming here. It's a pity I'm just staying overnight or until my clothes dry out! But I'm leaving for Whanganui tomorrow, and hopefully, the winds will have died down."

"Boy, that's a trip with the weather we've got. We're now in the tail-end of Cyclone Fehi today, but the south got it worse. Last night with the blue moon they got flooded up on the northern part of the South Island. A woman I know who lives down by Tasman Bay had her house flooded and ruined last night. She's got no fridge or cooker now!"

I look out of the window to the drenched bike and see the storm's rains are still battering down, giving little visibility over the misty neighbouring hills. Someone behind the bar turns the radio up: "New Zealand is declared a state of emergency along its West Coast, Queensland and down to Dunedin as the ferocious storm sweeps across the country packing huge winds. Cyclone Fehi is expected to create significant flooding and wind damage to many parts of the country with more heavy rain tonight. Wellington has cancelled all harbour ferries this afternoon. But the storm will move away overnight and tomorrow."

Four hours later, thoroughly warmed up, I notice three dishevelled travellers walk into the bar. One of them looks over to me and strangely smiles. Then with a beer in his hand he walks over. I have no idea who this person is but he seems to know me!

With a strong, stilted Alemannic accent he puts out his hand to shake mine, "I'm Samson Ming. And you're the girl on the bike, and you're here. I'm so happy you got here safe."

I nod in recognition, "Oh my god, you're the people who had that accident next to me. I'm so sorry I couldn't stop, but I was having my own problems."

"Yes, we saw. We've had quite a day too!"

I click my beer glass against his bottle, "I'd love to hear all about it to reassure myself I wasn't the only one who's gone through hell."

Putting his hands close to the burning fire and rubbing them together, Samson starts in stilted English, "Well, it was early this morning at a friend's house. I woke up a couch surfer to get the third travel mate I needed to share the ride and pitch in on gas for our trip down to New Plymouth. I'd already been here travelling quite a while from Switzerland. We were three people who'd never met before, driving on this beautiful rainy day and where you could barely see the cattle seeking shelter under the trees. I realize when I tell people about my crazy life they're often shocked, so I have a habit now of asking others about theirs.

"So I was curious and asked each girl to tell me something crazy or life changing. The girl from the Netherlands told me about her travels in Australia, while the German girl, Julia, said she'd never had something happen in her life!

"So after a while, I offered Julia to drive to get used to left-side driving. With my words *don't kill us!*, she started. It was raining heavy and rocks were sometimes on the road. The bigger ones we stopped to put them away on the side. Then we came to the gravel road. Julia had done pretty good and enjoyed the driving. So I thought I'd let her drive on the gravel."

He smiles from the memory, drinks some more beer and continues, "We came around the corner where we saw you, a poor motorcyclist trying to get going on the road. I was saying to Julia if she could maybe stop then we could help you get lighter and get your big bags into the car and drop them off at the hotel. But in that moment Julia overtook you, and in a second we were sitting sideways in the car!

"After getting out of the car, I realized we had sunk deeper into the mud, which already covered nearly half of the car. I realized quickly we weren't in a good position with all the rain, and I told the girls to collect rocks and place them under the wheels while I tried to dig out as much mud as possible to get the wheels a little free. One hour passes and no traffic passes. And no possibility to get out, with little progress. Now Julia is completely sad and I feel bad, as she's in my care, and the Netherland girl is not really happy. I tried to keep the mood up and said, 'At least you didn't kill us, and now you have a story to tell back home!' Then I smile, but not for long, as a car passes but with no rope. But they promise to tell someone in the next place that we need help. Yes it's true! Two hours pass while we're always trying to flatten the sides of the road and putting stones under the wheels until a backpackers' van comes along. With me pushing from behind, we finally get the car out. Wheels and engine are filled with mud, so I drive slowly to check all is good and then meet you here!" With that he takes a long swig from his bottle.

I almost feel I need to clap at the story-telling performance he's so eloquently described in his non-mother tongue, but just sit back in this safe sanctuary relieved for us all.

Peering through my curtains the next morning, with the welcome smell of dry clothes, I gulp in disbelief. The storm's disappeared, leaving a bright blue sky with the warm misty sun's rays pouring down and drying the roads. I gleefully, and perhaps a little childishly, clap my hands together. I head downstairs smiling for a well-deserved breakfast and enter a room full of OAP travellers. A younger motorcycle-clad guy standing in the queue behind me casually asks where I'm going. Without knowing who he is, I tell him about the hell I had on the mud-drenched gravel yesterday. He casually replies, saying that shouldn't have been a problem, as it's only twelve kilometres long! I almost swallow my toast! I later learn, seeing him eat with a group of American motorcyclists, that he's their tour leader. That probably confirms why I don't want to go with groups, with all that pressure.

I gaze across from where the bike's parked and notice a small colonial cottage on the corner of the quiet empty road that sweeps around into green woodland. From there, I take a small wander along the road to breathe in the clean mountain air and get my thoughts together for the next leg of this stretch of the Forgotten Highway. My Ghost Rider buddy has somehow now vanished indefinitely, so decisions and choices are now solely up to me. I'm hoping all will be well. And there on the opposite side of the road appears an unremarkable, old dilapidated garage door but with a hand painted anonymous message that could strangely almost have been written for me, but which strengthens my resolve—

Our deepest fear is not that we are inadequate.

Our deepest fear is that we are powerful beyond measure.

It is our light, not our darkness that most frightens us.

You playing small does not serve the world.

There is nothing enlightened about shrinking so that other people will not feel insecure around you.

We are all meant to shine as children do.

It is not just in some of us.

It is in everyone and as we let our own light shine,

We unconsciously give others permission to do the same.

As we are liberated from our fears, our presence automatically liberates others."

Marching briskly back, I confidently pull on my helmet and start the engine. This is going to be a wonderful day! The only important decision I've got to make today is whether to make a northbound diversion at Stratford and ride up and around the peninsula to New Plymouth and get a closer view of Mount Taranaki along The Surf Highway 45, or indicate left and head southbound straight to Whanganui. Here up in the mountains the storm and winds have moved on, but I'm only going to decide when I get to the junction at Stratford.

Clean, flat black asphalt welcomes me back onto the Forgotten Highway as I smoothly meander around the quiet roads bordered by the emerald green fields and hills on either side. No one is pushing me from the back. I have this beautiful place all to myself. The only vehicular life I later see along the way is a humongous bright red three decker, double trailer transporter lorry that has stopped at the gate of a field to load sheep.

Just before the "almost can't see" settlement of Douglas, I arrive at a high outlook with majestic panoramic views stretching out and across the fertile pastures and wooded terrain with layers upon layers of green mountain ridges disappearing into the far horizon. So spectacular are these views that I have to stop. It's also here I give another tick to those items my Maori friend had mentioned all those weeks ago in Heathrow and see a "Taranaki gate," or more like just a makeshift wire and batten gate named after the dairying area close by. This one is stretched between two wooden posts and has a barbed-wire top and five plain wires, which means when not used as a gate, it forms part of the fence. A few moments later, a couple parks up, get out of the car, and walks towards me. Mel, the wife, is from England, and Burt is from Australia. They stand next to me also looking out in awe.

Mel chirps up, "Isn't this a wonderful place? Not like back home. There're real problems in the UK, and we wouldn't live there now. But Australia, that's becoming the same. Would you like a photo taken with you in this incredible place?"

I nod, and although I've still got a black eye from the sailing mishap, I happily smile into the camera and then wave them goodbye.

The ride down to Stratford is painless as I park up on the main street lined with old dilapidated art deco shop fronts, to finally make a decision on which direction to take. Although the clouds are starting to come in and there was a bit of a drizzle earlier, it's still relatively dry, and more importantly, there's not much wind. So that ticks a few boxes. There's not much traffic riding through the main thoroughfare of Broadway, except for a massive logging lorry piled high with giant tree trunks and then a truck pulling a ship's container proudly emblazoned on its sides with "Hooker Pacific!" I'll take the risk and see how far north I can get. If it worsens, then I'll simply just head back inland and avoid the Taranaki Peninsula's coastal road.

The petrol station attendant nods when I tell him where I'm planning to go. "Really? You be careful now! The wind's already picking up. It's all got to do with that damn blue moon. That coast road south from Plymouth is gonna be dangerous."

I seriously digest what he's said but still ride north to see if I can at least view Mount Taranaki. I twist the throttle and, after a few miles, quickly looking down at the map, take a leftie off onto a small rural rain-sodden road. After fifteen or twenty so kilometres, out on the horizon and covered in clouds I have my first glimpse of the famed Mount Taranki in the Egmont National Park. But I'm saddened to see that at least two thirds of this 2,518 metre high mountain is totally obscured by low lying cloud. The wind has now become threateningly strong, and it's here, for my safety, that I reluctantly decide not to continue any further up and around this stretch of coast, but to head back. From what I've seen and heard, there seems no real sense in it. Reluctantly, I turn the bike round and, looking into my mirror, now notice the mystical mountain has totally disappeared from sight.

Approaching Normanby, and now mentally crossing my legs, I'm on the lookout to find a toilet or somewhere to stop and relieve myself. The Normanby Racecourse appears on my left, and with its gates open and a little yellow coffee trailer parked up inside, I signal and ride in next to it. Lene, a smiling blonde bespectacled lady, leans over the counter and beckons me over.

"Morning. What kind of coffee can I do you?"

"Thanks, but I'm first just going to take a little wander to check out this place."

That's my excuse. I waddle past and round the corner where a circular grass race track appears with a row of empty stables facing it. Looking around to see no one's watching, I nip inside one and give out a sigh of relief. That feels better. A perfect hot coffee is ready when I get back, and at this point a dungareed Maori steps out of a van and introduces himself as Clem, the husband to Lene.

"So is there anything worthwhile seeing before I hit Whanganui later on?"

Clem smiles like he's got a bit of inside info, "There sure is! You'll be biking through Waverly. Go stop and see the old clock tower. Parliament did something crazy a few months back and changed the law. Normally, one guy simply climbs up the stairs to wind the clock up every six days. But due to damn Health and Safety and the act that just went through, he now needs a volunteer to stand by the door in case there's a problem, or else it has to be converted to an electronic clock! So where did you say you've come from?"

"Well I didn't, but I've just aborted going up to New Plymouth and getting up close to Mount Taranaki. As you know, the weather could be better."

"Well, you'll see Whanganui feels a lot different to the rest of the North Island. There's an old fashioned charm and slow pace to it, like the pace of its river. The Whanganui River is very special and the country's longest watercourse. Due to legend, the river is seen as being very important in the lives of the Maori. It's so significant to us that the New Zealand government has given it recognition as a 'living person'! And this month, in February 2018, the government will also announce the sacred Mount Taranaki as another 'living person'. The Maori don't like people standing on the mountain because it's like standing on someone's head and very disrespectful. Yes, of course people will still be able to climb it, but more respect is needed, like not dropping any litter. We, the Maori, believe that anything providing food, weather, and vegetation should be looked after."

I nod in reverence to him. I'm handed another coffee and, after a while chatting, trot back to the stable and then promptly set off again. The coastal road to Waverly passes without incident, and I curiously stop the bike in front of the tall white clock tower when I reach this quiet "like nothing's happening" place to stare upwards at it. At that very moment my phone buzzes from under my jacket, and I curiously take it out.

It's a short message from Samson: "Hi. On the road to New Plymouth, and just now the rain was so hard that I could barely see ten metres. The wind beat my car, almost breaking the window, and I was amazed that we didn't have another accident!"

My heart skips a beat, hoping they're alright and feeling relieved I'd decided with a sixth sense to turn back. I had nothing to prove to anybody. It sounds stupid, but what I'd experienced just yesterday was starting to make me feel just a bit stressed, due to the unexpected conditions of these roads. Maybe I'm being paranoid, with no one travelling with me to give reassurance and support, but all of a sudden I'm feeling the roads may turn to dirt like the nightmare yesterday. Stupid but true.

I stroll into a café opposite the clock and sit on a stool at the counter hungrily looking at which scrummy cake I'm going to choose. Once again, a smiling woman is leaning over from the other side interested to hear what I've been doing and how the trip's progressing.

But I'm also interested to learn more about what's really happening in New Zealand, so I put out an open ended statement, "There's a hell of a lot of diversity here in your country from one place to the next. Wealthy areas and poorer places. But I'm finding it quite expensive ... "

She slowly stirs her cup of tea in this empty café. "Yea. If you look around and get under the skin of the place, you'll see we've got our own problems like everywhere else in the world. Where do I start? Well, first of all you've got to realize that there're a lot of problems with alcoholism here. The government is trying to get people not to buy alcohol and have the country smoke-free by 2030. Everyone smokes, and some people's children just don't wear shoes because of the parents' choices. It's crazy with the high price points for this stuff with a heavy tax put on them. It's hard to believe, but the cheapest pack of twenty is twenty-six dollars and ninety dollars for a fifty-gram drum of tobacco. And the next tax-year in March 2019 will see twenty cigarettes at thirty dollars! Alcohol is just as badly taxed. It's sixty-six dollars for a 750-gram bottle of Baileys, sixty-six to seventy-five dollars for Grand Marnier, when it's something like ten Euros in Italy, a good gin like Tanqueray a hundred dollars or Gordons at eighty-nine dollars. It's crazy."

She ardently continues, "And boy, how we eat. So many people eat Kentucky Fried Chicken 'cos it's cheaper than supermarket food. So with all this there's a lot of socio-economic depression, and it feels like the government's sponsoring it. You hear these crazy stories. Just the other day, nearby, a single eighteen-year-old mother with a child was given, just like that, a $12,000 Mazda 6, and you hear stories about doctors prescribing drugs like morphine after surgery that the patients then get addicted to."

She sighs then chuckles out loud, "But hell, New Zealand is a great place, and we've all just got to get on with it to make changes for the better."

Looking out of the café's tied-back curtained windows, the spitting rain has stopped, so I pull on my jacket and wish my new friend success in all her ventures as I walk out of the door onto the quiet street.

HERD OF BULLS.....BULLOCKS?

BULLS
BOLLOCKS

YOU CAN HANG YOUR HAT ON THEM!

10

WHAT A LOAD OF BULL!

SAVAGE CLUB—GREEN PARROTS—BIKES GALORE

It's just another couple of days until I'm back in Wellington to catch the ferry to the South Island and race down to its very tip to catch the famous Burt Munro Challenge races and festivities. But at this very moment, as I ride alongside the slow pace of the calming giant Whanganui River it somehow seems to mirror image the feeling of this charming, old fashioned town of Whanganui. It immediately gives me the impression of peaceful remoteness and being in the middle of nowhere. But this had been an important place due to the river's access to the ports of Wellington and New Plymouth for early European trade. Today it's a lot quieter, and this morning all I can see floating on the waters and moored to the sides are a large river steamer and a few small motorboats.

And it's here on Somme Parade that I park outside the historic building of Tamara Lodge, popular with backpackers and independent travellers, where I'll be spending the night. I'm led into a large comfortable room all to myself overlooking the river.

Although the bike's parked out on the street, the whole place feels so sedate that I really don't think there'll be a problem with its security tonight.

The rest of the day will be spent just chilling, catching the vibe, and resting before biking down to the outskirts of Wellington tomorrow. And it's already starting to brighten up after this morning's 200 kilometre manic and eclectic ride from the interior on the mountainous Forgotten Highway. I'm happy to have nothing planned, except to maybe find a half decent place for a late lunch and then meander around aimlessly. Before long, I'm digging into tender lamb and drinking a chilled Dusky Sounds Chardonnay. The table next to me at the Stellar Bar also has a fellow traveller looking at the integral piece of reading material, a worn out weather-beaten map. Something gives away his mode of transport, as a motorcycle helmet is on the chair next to him.

I look over and smile, pointing at the green full-face helmet, "Looks like you're travelling on a bike? Me too."

The blonde-haired guy with a red bandana tied round his neck and a strong Aussie accent smiles back. "Yea, a handful of weeks. But it's the extreme weather that's surprised me most. Hot and humid with sick record-breaking temperatures, then the very next minute heavy rain and gale force winds with that cyclone!"

I nod, totally understanding, "Tell me about it. I rode in from Stratford today, missing the 45. I felt like a bit of a wimp."

His eyes widen. "Now listen here! You were not! That coast road had 140 kilometre-an-hour winds today from the tail end of the cyclone. When I heard that, I shit a brick. Glad I wasn't there. It's very unusual, and yea, you would have been crazy to do that sea road. I met another biker a few weeks ago who'd broken both arms out on the roads. They're f . . . ing good roads, but goddamn, you gotta be careful."

Wiping his mouth with his serviette and picking up his helmet to leave he adds, "It's Friday, so if you get a chance, check out the Savage Club tonight for some live music."

What a little beauty this place is with its late Victorian and Edwardian decorative building façades, well-tended streets, art galleries, glassworks, museums including the majestic hilltop Sarjeant Gallery in Queen's Park but currently closed for earthquake strengthening, and even the 1899 white opera house.

There's one place in the world that I'm reminded of and that's when I travelled to Manaus in the Brazilian rainforest. They could almost be sister towns with their opera houses and for that lost, laid-back feel. To get a better perspective of the place, I walk over the river, through a Maori-carved gateway into a 213-metre tunnel and up the historic 1919 Durie Hill Elevator, which comes out onto the hillside. The views are spectacular out and across the city, with the river meandering alongside, but even better when I climb next to it, the further 176 steps up the Memorial Tower and to the highest point in the city.

That night, I walk the silent, unlit streets up and along Queens Park to the Savage Club Hall. Stepping through the wooden doors of this old tin-clad building and paying just ten dollars, I'm transported back in time to see families of all ages sitting side by side around long trestle tables tapping their feet and clicking their fingers to the beat of the musicians up on stage. But it's the wall décor I'm also mesmerized by. The place is lined with Maori influenced woodwork panelling and sculptures with old black and white photographs of musicians hanging in the shadowy recesses.

This place was originally the Whanganui Savage Club formed in 1891. The original Savage Club began as a gentleman's club in London in 1857 and spread to have branches around the colonial world. It was essentially a literary society and became an entertainment club where members would put on musical performances and sketches. Only in 1998 were women allowed to join the club! Unfortunately, due to a declining and ageing membership here, the club closed in 2016 and the building's ownership was transferred to the Whanganui Musicians Club. It's so good to see this atmospheric, vibey-as-hell venue with its art and history lining the walls still performing.

I sit next to a couple of local musicians tightening their guitar and violin strings with one pointing over to the stage, "We've also got Dave Flynn, the Irish player, up tonight. Should go down well."

Still tapping my feet, I leave the Club later that evening, out onto the empty streets, continuing to hear the music hollering out and following me all the way down the hill.

Early next morning, I ride along the empty Taupo Quay, where only the local artisans, and fruit and vegetable growers are setting up their stalls for the weekly market. I park up next to a little van by the river serving me fresh coffee and a pastry or two. But I'm already feeling the need to quickly move on, due to my concerns about the forecasted weather and the unknown 190-kilometre journey down to Paekakariki, my final base before catching the boat the day after. But I needn't have worried so much. I cross relatively flat plains and grasslands for about thirty kilometres until I reach one place I certainly wanted to stop and take a browse around.

Bulls is a small roadside settlement, and I begin to understand why it attracts so much attention. Everything has something to do with the animal, the Bull, using amusing connotations left, right, and centre. I park up next to a massive bull wall mural to take a closer look. Already, a large black bull sculpture stands outside the fire station with the sign "Extinguish-A-Bull". And it just goes on as I walk along the pavement; the dairy shop, "Bulls Avail-A-Bull"; the bakery with the animals displayed in the window with chefs' hats on;, the medical centre, "Cure-A-Bull"; the pharmacy, "Indispense-A-Bull"; the chiropractic, "Adjust-A-Bull"; the estate agents, "Lease-A-Bull"; and so it continues down the street outside the Town Hall, "Socio-A-Bull"; the library, "Read-A-Bull"; and the butchers, "What a load of Bull".

As is becoming customary, I stop to strike up a friendly banter with one of the town's café owners, this time Di, to find out what's going on around here. She's another strong, passionate woman who doesn't mince her words, "Ah you know, some of the New Zealanders here are just a bit arrogant because everything is becoming global, so it's dog eat dog like with the Americans and Europeans. I'm half Maori, and even I feel the racial undercurrent. But it's also how we get to communicate with the next generation and our kids. It's difficult with their behaviour, as the only way they seem to know how to communicate is online. Kids nowadays don't like face-to-face dialogue."

By this time, Di's smiling giant Maori husband has casually wandered in, and listening to our conversation, he nods, "Yea, I agree. Even I get a hard time sometimes, but I'm so jealous you're heading to the Burt Munro. That's something I've always wanted to do."

Di chirps in, "Hell, we wish you well. And on a lighter note, which I'm sure will make you smile and for use as a bit of family trivia back home, did you know that Bulls and Cowes on the Isle of Wight are twin towns?"

We all burst out laughing, and stuffing a few pies into my tank bag, I'm off again down the road leaving warm, kind, and friendly people. It's also here I leave Highway 3 and jump south onto Highway 1 for another 112 kilometres. I'm still being battered around a bit by the sporadic gusts of wind racing across the plains and blowing over the highway, but what I am noticing is the increasing visibility of urban sprawl. The first place I come to is the little town of Otaki, probably known more for its rural railway station and definitely worth a stop. I squeeze and back in between two cars along the busy high street and walk to the picturesque little station, which looks out over to the mountains.

It was originally built in 1886 as part of the Manawatu line as a passenger service for 600 travellers. This changed the place totally as the station became a centre of commerce for almost a hundred years, being the link between the town and the outside world. It was a trading stop, post office, and café. In the years after World War II, a burgeoning market garden industry made the station a hive of activity. Several times a week gardeners brought their produce to the rail yards to load onto the wagons. Trucks lined up with tomatoes, pumpkins, cabbage, and other produce bound for the markets in Wellington, Palmerston North, Whanganui, Napier, and New Plymouth.

But today the only train that stops here is the morning Capital Connection train from Palmerston North carrying commuters to Wellington and back again in the evening. Currently, the local community and district council are trying to restore it back to regular rail service. That would certainly help keep some of the cars off the roads here in this busy area.

Continuing through the now permanent urban sprawl and riding parallel to the same railway line I finally turn off, bump over a set of tracks and into the tiny little seaside town of Paekakari meaning "the perching place of the green parakeet."

I smile at the coincidence, as this reminds me of back home where I see them flying all over the place! The story back in the UK goes that some were brought into the nearby film studios in Isleworth, where the jungle scenes were being created for the set of the *African Queen* with Katherine Hepburn and Humphrey Bogart. After the filming finished in the early 1950s these little green parrots began to arrive in the local gardens in West London. People then say that at the end of filming they released them all. No one still really knows where they came from, but there are other stories out there that include claims that Jimi Hendrix released a breeding pair in Carnaby Street in the 1960s. Amazingly, there are now around 8,600 breeding pairs of green tropical parrots throughout England, so they're not just here!

This place is the southern extent of the Kapiti Coast I've just come down, the narrow plain between the rugged and inhospitable Tararua Range and the Tasman breakers, littered with its commuter belt suburbs, beaches, and golf courses. With the little cafés dotted along a cabbage tree lined central road and their shorts and T-shirt clad people sipping cool drinks, this place certainly feels like a happy-go-lucky beach community.

Riding through a rural tree-lined street, I stop at the bottom of a hill, where a hidden house stands at the top of an Everest-like road for its steepness. I smile once again thinking about my Airbnb choice. But the hosts, Doris and a Swiss lady and her motorcyclist husband, Sam, can't be more welcoming as I walk up panting and sweating to knock on the front door.

Doris opens the door, rubbing white floury hands down her apron, "Ah Zoë, we're so pleased to see you. As we mentioned in our messages to you, we're having a party here tonight for one of our friends who's leaving to go to college in England. We'd love you to join us, and there'll be lots of food too. But we've so many people arriving and staying here tonight I do hope you won't mind just a bit of celebratory noise with some of our musician friends playing. Make yourself at home!"

That sounds good to me, and with that, Sam walks back down to the bike to help with the luggage

"Well gidday, Zoë. How's it going? Are you sure you wanna keep that big bike of yours down there? I know even we have difficulty getting up our driveway, but I could maybe help you get it up?"

Without hesitation, I shake my head smiling, "Ah, that's quite alright. I'll be leaving early tomorrow, so it'll be good to have it already out on the street to get to the ferry. And anyway, this road is pretty quiet."

"Yea, not much stuff happening here."

So after a little stroll along the high, rubbly walkway overlooking the Cook Strait and sitting against its wall to lap up the sun, I wander back into the small settlement and sit outside The Perching Parrot Café. I eat a small salmon salad for twenty-two dollars, which in my reckoning is pretty expensive all said and done. Anyway, with nothing much else to do and to while away the hours a bit until the evening, I inquisitively walk over the rails and onto the old station platform.

There's nobody else here except a bizarre lookalike Salvador Dalí with a long thin moustache and a red beret waiting patiently for a potentially surreal train, as nothing seems to be coming up the long, distant tracks. But there is a little museum and, surprisingly, a bookshop. I walk through the second door, and seated hidden behind a stack of books is an old white bearded guy wearing a Beatles T-shirt. He stands up to introduce himself as Michael O'Leary, the store owner, author, historian, and poet. This is yet another fascinating person with lots of stories, this time about the railways he worked on with the S9 track gang north of Dunedin in the 1990s.

"Yea, those years working on the railways for track maintenance on the South Island were interesting! But I've been here quite a while. Paekakari's first station was a vital part of New Zealand's longest and most successful private railway. In the 1870s the government bought Maori land for a west coast railway but stopped in 1878 when the economy slumped. Wellington businessmen decided to do the job themselves and formed the Wellington and Manawatu Railway Company. In exchange for building and operating the line, the government provided land along the route to sell. As you can imagine, this created a huge response, and a line of new towns set among farms was created along the foothills. And there you go, the region was transformed!"

He continues piling books up on the counter, "So you see, everything changed here for the better. From the time people first came here, there was only one way to travel up and down the coast and that was to follow the beach. Nearly all Maori Kainga, or settlements, were built in the dunes at the mouth of a stream. From the 1840s, Pakeha as well as Maori walked or rode along the beach— mail carriers, settlers with their livestock, troops and civil servants, Maori taking produce to sell in Wellington. And we had former whalers open pubs at river crossings and provide a ferry service. Amazingly later in the 1860s scheduled horse coach services ran along the beach between Wellington and Whanganui!"

As the sun starts to lower, I walk back to the house to find it's become a hive of activity. Handfuls of people are placing massive plates of food on a large table and helping Doris bring even more sustenance from the kitchen. I step out onto the picturesque terrace looking out to sea, where dozens of other people are already chattering away and pushing a glass of wine into my hand. Later that evening, and all sat on the floor or on chairs forming a circle, everyone offers their own performances of poems, music, or stories to wish the young Kiwi traveller a safe and exciting trip to the other side of the world.

Walking downstairs the next morning, there are still a handful of hungover looking people camped out on the floor. Unsurprisingly, Doris is busy kneading dough and preparing food as I walk into the kitchen. "Morning Zoë. I've just made some homemade sourdough bread, muesli, and yoghurt. Help yourself and please make a sandwich to take with you to Wellington."

Later on, Sam kindly carries the bag down and helps tie it back onto the bike. "Now remember. You've got plenty of time before you catch the boat at 2:45PM, and it's only about forty kilometres, so shouldn't take you more than an hour. But be careful to look out for the ferry terminal signs and exit, which is a left turn down the steep descent well before you get into Wellington proper. Good luck and happy travels."

And with that, I'm off. Without putting it too mildly, considering what I've already experienced, this is a doddle along Highway 1 today. There's a bright blue summer sky without any wind, plus it's a Sunday morning so a lot quieter without the weekday commuters heading into the capital. I've almost forgotten what it feels like not to be battered around!

As I ride into the port area, the atmosphere is already completely different from when I'd first arrived a month ago with just myself and two other motorcycles getting off. Today, it's buzzing. There are already large groups of bikes of all descriptions, models, and engine sizes from racers, Harleys, Indian tourers, Triumphs, and Japanese brands parked up in front of me waiting to board. I also park up, taking my place in the enormous queue and take a look around. All the bikes have something in common. They're all loaded and packed with bags and luggage for at least a handful of days, which means they're going some distance. They're all with New Zealand number plates, and everyone I hear and talk to are from the North Island. They can only be going to one place.

And the guys and gals standing next to me confirm this: "Yea, we're all making our way down to Invercargill to get there by midweek before it all starts on Thursday. This for us is the big one, taking time off from work and riding down to the bottom of the South Island to see the best racers and party all weekend!"

In my estimations there must be somewhere between at least three to four hundred bikes. It's getting increasingly warmer as we patiently wait, standing by the bikes or strolling over to inquisitively look at other people's machines, and most of us have already stripped off our jackets and tied them down. There's a raw feeling of excitement and anticipation in waiting to be beckoned to board the large ship. Then all of a sudden we see the signal and are told that due to the numbers the bikes have been given priority to get on first before the four-wheel vehicles. Everyone jumps into action, pulling helmets and gloves on, and starting the hundreds of bikes up that have now formed a giant line. The sound is deafening. The deep, loud rumbling and droning sound of the engines is mesmerizing as slowly each bike starts to move forward.

My initial fear of uncontrollable balance due to the bike's weight is unfounded as I steadily ride the Bonnie up the steep ramp, over the knobbly steel floor, through and into the belly of the InterIslander ship. The sight is quite spectacular, seeing the hundreds of bikers follow me one by one and starting to park in rows and rows throughout the hull. It reminds me of the boat trip I'd made last year from Liverpool to get to the Isle of Man for the TT Races with, again, a massive ship full of bikes!

I manage to get a prime spot by the wall and reading the sign "Caution Deck Slippery, Take Care!", I carefully bring the bike to a stop, leave it in gear, push a big rubber stop behind the back wheel, and tie the bike down securely to the floor with my straps. But without hesitation I ask one of the bikers next to me to just double-check what I've done, and after a quick once-over, he smiles putting his thumbs up. We all march up the stairs into the ship, and I rush up onto the top level-three deck to watch all the cars, campervans, and lorries now also slowly drive in. I can't believe that today is just one

of a handful of times that I've experienced almost perfect weather since covering almost 4,000 kilometres over the past four weeks. The weather has been exceptionally extreme from the post cyclones and torrential storms to some of the hottest summer weather New Zealand has ever recorded. The crossing will take three hours before I arrive in Picton this evening, then with just a short ride down to a vineyard to indulge in a couple of glasses of strong, palatable wine. So here we go! Bring it on!

PART TWO

THE SOUTH ISLAND

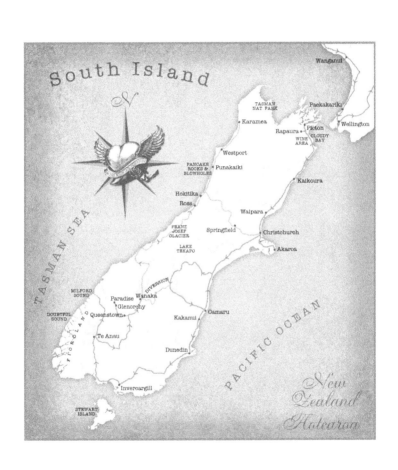

11

Abandoned in a Vineyard

Tyres crushing Grapes—Train Carriage Hospitality—Sandfly bites

The mountainous northern shores of the South Island are coming into eyesight as three dolphins suddenly appear and playfully swim with our boat all the way to Picton. You can feel the anticipation in the air. Hundreds of bikers are excitedly getting ready, putting their gear back on, and untying their bikes as the boat slowly moors up. As the back-end of the stern is lowered, the engines start up into one harmonious gigantic roar.

I'm also ready to go, patiently following all the other leather and jean clad bikers down the ramp and out into the late afternoon sunshine. Everyone is speeding away with no time to lose, and before long, I'm all on my own riding down Route 1, better known here as the Classic New Zealand Wine Trail. Due to the alternative road I'd taken to get to Picton via the Queen Charlotte Sound, I hadn't ridden this section but was pleasantly surprised by its smooth flatness and, before long, Blenheim was appearing and I was heading inland to Rapaura.

There's no question that this is the heart of Marlborough, the country's most celebrated and largest wine growing region. Hailed as one of New Zealand's most sunny and dry regions, Maori referred to this Wairau Valley as "Kei Puta te Wairau"—"The place with the Hole in the Cloud."

The region's famed Sauvignon blanc, alone, is planted across 44,000 acres of this massive land of vineyards, which is fascinating to think about when you stop to consider that all of the Napa Valley in California has a total of 45,000 acres planted for the entirety of its wine production. Some even say Marlborough country produces the best Sauvignon blanc in the world.

And very soon I'm riding through row upon row of endless green vineyards sprawling out into the distance to the edge of the faraway mountains. I'd remembered the name of the lane, as it was my maiden name, Matthews, and had booked a room at a little place in the middle of these delicious vineyards. I look down at the tank bag with the note under the plastic cover that my hosts had sent: "At Spring Creek turn right and keep on until the big Matua winery, turn left into Jacksons Road and when you arrive at the corner of Cloudy Bay turn left and we're the entrance between the two palm trees."

The quiet, empty road stretches out until I smile and turn left onto little Matthews Lane. I'm smiling because I'm also passing possibly one of the most famous of the wineries—Cloudy Bay—which even

I know of and have drunk one or more glasses of in my local pub! The place looks like a massive, smooth operation, and passing by I notice a sign beckoning people to come in for wine tasting with its own gourmet restaurant. I'd been told to continue up a hundred or so metres, where there'd be a small house. But I see nothing. I come to a frustrated stop next to a couple of cottages to check I haven't gone too far.

A handsome, dark-haired guy in shorts comes out from one of the cottages and walks towards me casually asking, "Bonjour Mademoiselle, are you alright? Are you looking for something?"

I smile, recognising the strong French accent. "I'm not quite sure. I'm supposed to have found a house, number 78."

He scratches his sexy stubbled chin in thought, "Ah, oui, oui, oui! No problem. It's a bit further with the palm trees. I'm Alex, the Head Chef here at Oyster Bay. If you have a problem, you can always come back and crash out here in our cottage."

Now that is an invitation, and for once I was hoping I wasn't going to find number 78! We both cheekily smile, and I continue on. But past the wealth of Oyster Bay Winery, the road suddenly turns to a rubbly, slippery path. My favourite! But thankfully, just a little bit further up I notice two palm trees. I park the bike and wander up through the driveway to a little wooden one-storey chalet. The place is quiet, and all I can see are a handful of old, battered jeeps and massive piles of what I'd call junk.

Out of nowhere, a cheery guy appears, peddling a bicycle and pulling what looks like a one wheel box-trailer.

"Hi. Am I at 78? I've booked a room for the night."

He continues cycling in big circles around me. "Cristina, my wife, should be back at any minute from the café she cooks at. But she told me to show you the room. She also mentioned that you're more than welcome to eat with us this evening. Where's your luggage?"

"I was nervous riding up, so it's still on the bike down the road."

"Not a problem. By the way, I'm Simon. Jump into that blue jeep over there, and we'll grab it."

And with that, I push a pile of more junk away from the seat, leaving just enough room to squeeze onto its edge. Justifying my initial statement I add, "I've got another early start tomorrow, so I'll probably leave the bike there."

"Yea, we'll just push the bike between those vines, out of sight, and so you can also easily ride out. Shouldn't be a problem."

Shortly after, I follow Simon into the house, which has a high spire church-like ceiling, but again, the space is chock-a-blocked with piles of boxes, dusty broken furniture, old fashioned photocopiers, stacks of cables, an aeroplane passenger seat, and hundreds of other pieces of paraphernalia. There must be a story here!

The bag is dumped onto a bed overlooking vineyards and a golden setting sun. It's dark by the time I hear a car, and a pretty girl walks into the house. She greets me by kissing both my cheeks, and with a strong Italian accent smiles, "Welcome to our humble abode. Let's go to the kitchen and pour some wine while I prepare some Italian food from my native town of Bologna. We're renting this place at the moment, but the vineyard owners have said we have to move out next month, so it's pretty crazy."

I don't know why, but I already like these kind, honest people. There's some sort of raw, natural feel to the way they're living. Before long, mouth-watering lamb in a rich Italian sauce and pasta are being generously dished out onto plates, and Cristina finally sits down. She looks exhausted. We raise our glasses, and all hungrily tuck in.

After a short silence, the conversation naturally flows, jumping from one topic to the other. Wiping my mouth with the serviette I smile, "That bicycle you rode earlier is so cool, being able to pull stuff."

Simon nods and helps himself to more pasta. "Well you know, people must think I'm a bit eccentric, but here you've got to become self-sufficient to survive. I go and collect a lot of stuff people just don't want and make money from it. That bike and trailer, I paid just eight dollars for from the local "Re-use Shop," where a lot of unwanted but usable stuff is sold back to the public. All this stuff I've got I've found at dumps, tips, and recycling places. A lot of it costs nothing. You saw that red car out front on the grass? There was nothing wrong with it; it even had a tank full of petrol; and cost me fifty dollars! People around here are very wealthy and are getting rid of stuff all the time, including expensive clothes we find at charity shops."

"And Cristina, do you like it here?"

"Well, we both met a few years ago in Italy and moved back here, as it's where Simon's from, but that's a hot question. Of course, because I'm with Simon, but there are problems. I work very hard as a chef in one of the local cafés, and I see it."

"What do you see?"

"Well, I sometimes feel uncomfortable. There's not a very good feel from the locals' perception of foreigners living here. It's not towards the foreign tourists that come here, as they get respect, but directed to the people who live here permanently. Just the other day I was selling some of my produce at the market and a lady asked where I came from. I told her Italy. And she simply said, "So why don't you go back there?" I was shocked and hurt. There's definitely some xenophobia in this area. And people here are generally not used to new things. Last week I went to the market again to sell and cook some of the tortellini I'd made, and I had to bring my own friends along to start tasting it or no one else would have tried them. Most bizarre!

"An Australian friend recently told me that New Zealanders are maybe not ready for my Italian food and style of cooking. It hurts me, but we keep trying, as we both love this place."

It's getting late, and everyone looks tired, with Simon finally looking at his watch, "We're both leaving early tomorrow for work, so put your bag outside your door, and I'll drop it next to the bike, and you can take your time to have some breakfast before you go. Just pull the door behind you."

I wake up to an amber and orange sunrise painting the emerald green vineyards outside my window. The bag outside my door has already disappeared as I walk into the kitchen. I notice Cristina's kindly left me a pot of fresh coffee ready to be filled with hot water and some fresh bread with homemade strawberry jam. Next to it all is a little handwritten message: "Ciao Zoe! Hope you had a good night sleep. Help yourself to anything you need. Here is a present for you and your trip to the South . . . Blood sucking sandflies could be really annoying and this healing balm of kukni, tamanu, lavender and Manuka honey I make will relieve the itchiness of the bites! Enjoy New Zealand, Cristina xx"

Carrying my helmet and tank bag, I walk back down the uneven, rubbly path and see Simon's kindly placed the heavy bag on the back of the bike's seat, which is parked close to their green post box. I reckon to reach Waipara, which is close to Christchurch, and another well-known wine producing area, I'll be clocking up around 260 kilometres. But looking at the forecast, it's already predicting more strong winds with a possible new storm coming in later. So once again, needing to navigate through the treacherous earthquake hit roads around Kaikoura, it's imperative I get started to cover as much distance as quickly as possible.

Without much choice, I was coming back today on the same stretch of coastal road I'd already been on in the first few days of the trip, but which seems like an age ago. I ride the bike out from behind the grapevines, and slowly accelerating, I'm off. Riding in the opposite direction of any road always looks and feels different, and this dramatic sea-lined landscape was no exception with views you'd never tire of. As I was eating up the kilometres, the winds were coming back to haunt me and becoming, in my humble opinion, more and more treacherous in the way they were knocking me mercilessly back and forth. I clench my teeth, pray to my travelling spirits for a safe journey, tuck my head down, and just try hard to keep up a steady pace.

The only other motorcyclist I see along the way is an old guy near Clarence, who funnily enough, had stopped at the same time in a layby as a touring cyclist, making me amusingly envisage they were travelling together.

Just 130 kilometres south of Kaikoura along the earthquake destroyed road, and with a hefty 264 kilometres already notched up today, I finally get to a junction with SH7 leading to Hanmer Springs, marking the beginning of one of New Zealand's fastest growing wine regions. It's here I indicate to turn off, ride across a bumpy railway track, along a little parallel country road dotted with pretty small farm houses and barns, and to the teeny settlement of Waipara that with one blink would be gone. The place is totally deserted of human life. But it's not the vineyards I've come to see, it's an unusual hidden away place to lie my head down for the night.

And with the wind just about to knock me off, I couldn't have arrived at a better time as I ride into the tree lined Waipara Sleepers campsite. But it's not just tents here, it's also old train carriages that have been faithfully restored for the weary traveller.

On a cold but clear mid-winter's day in 1990, three guards vans finally left the main NZR line, which is now privately run by Tranz Rail, for their new home. Towed up from Christchurch on the end of an overnight freight train, they were shunted onto the siding here in Waipara village. Their fifty-year career, which had started in the 1940s, had ended carrying the Guard and the mail throughout the South Island. It's estimated they must have travelled a massive 2.4 million kilometres each, or 50,000 kilometres each year.

So yes, this place is certainly quirky as I park up by a wall painted with a whistle-blowing station master and a hole in the wall ticket office. An intercom button is next to it, which I push.

From around a corner, a guy in the mandatory wellies and cropped shorts and looking more like a sheep farmer, ambles over sticking his hand out to strongly shake mine.

"Well gidday. What can we do for you?"

"I've booked a train carriage. Is it ready?"

He chuckles, "Well for sure. It's our special double carriage, which I'll do you a deal for fifty dollars. Come and take a look."

We walk over, and I smile with glee seeing a red and green painted carriage surrounded by lavender bushes. We walk up a few steps from the back into a narrow carriage with just enough room for a small TV hanging from the wall, a tiny fridge on the floor with a toaster and kettle on the top, a small armchair, and cupboard. Peering into the next part of the white wooden-lined carriage, I see it's totally acceptable, with a comfortable looking squeezed-in double bed with an old fashioned ornately decorated metal headboard. There are even small curtains around all the windows and lots of old pictures and photographs of Waipura. But my smile broadens as I see hanging seriously on the wall the one necessity we all need, and that's a tractor calendar showing exciting images of different tractors for each month. This makes me think that, like so many other people I've met, that he's also maybe a farmer.

"So will this do you? The camp kitchen and washing facilities are on the other side of the site, where you might see a few other people."

"You bet! All I need now is to find some food. I've only got a pack of dry pasta."

"Well there's nothing much here. But you may wanna walk down to the village store. They'll probably sell you some pies and veg."

"Cheers, I'll do that. This really is a great place."

"Yea, me and my wife, Fiona, love it. But I'm really a sheep farmer with a place up in the hills. Which reminds me, I've gotta dash back to the farm. But before I do that, I've gotta tell you I'm worried scared that the wind is gonna knock your bike over. We gotta protect it. Listen, let's get it up against your carriage, and if the worst comes to the worst, we'll try and lift it into the carriage!"

My eyes open wide in disbelief in what I've just heard, but the blue sky is ominously darkening, so I obligingly nod and we push the bike up closely against the side of the old carriage.

By now, my stomach is rumbling, so I set off along the little road and arrive at the Waipara Garden tin shack store with a pretty display of flowering plants on the shelves outside. I go to open the door, but it's locked. I push it to double-check. A scribbled note with a hand drawn smiley is taped to the door: "Monday 5th. Apologies but will be closed this PM. Just use Honesty Box."

Damn, this isn't good, as others must have had the same idea. All the shelves advertising fresh, delicious cucumbers, tomatoes, courgettes, and herbs are empty. There're only one lonely courgette and a box of eggs left, which I quickly grab and push a five-dollar note into the Honesty Box. On my way back, I stop and pick some apples from a roadside tree as extra sustenance. With the food carefully wrapped in my jumper, I walk up the steps into the little prefab kitchen where a slim, athletic guy wearing Lycra biking shorts is seated at a table intently reading a local newspaper.

He looks up and smiles, while I start preparing a little courgette omelette with pasta. "Hello. I'm Heinrich from Germany and sheltering here from the storm."

I also join in with a smile, "Hi, and I'm Zoë doing the same, also on two wheels but with an engine! I've come down from the north shore today, where the winds have been horrendous."

He nods totally understanding, not needing to hear any further explanation, "Yah, I agree. The wind has almost blown me off back to Germany! No exaggerating!"

I sit down opposite him and start tucking in. "So are you having a good time? I've just come over from the North Island where I was biking for a month, and I have to admit there were some difficult parts."

In his strong, to the point, German accent he replies, "Yah, I've already cycled 4,000 kilometres, but I feel it's not a great place anymore for two wheels. I first came here in 2005 and the roads were pretty quiet, and then ten years later it totally changed. And it's changing fast now. Many more tourists, trucks, cars racing past. It's dangerous!"

That night Paul, my host, had predicted correctly, and the storm continued to sweep in, but thankfully I am dry and cosy in my little train carriage. But to add to the merriment, I was now also continually itching from horrible sandfly bites. I stare into the mirror and, not for the first time, look with shock to see two massive, unflattering red lumps, one above my right eye and one in the centre of my forehead like a cyclops monster. To add to the joy, masses of red pimply bites are appearing all over my arms and legs. Dabbing the cream all over that Cristina had only just given me this morning, and which feels like a lifetime ago, tossing and turning I try to get some shuteye without itching my skin off!

12

MILKY WAY OVER MACKENZIE COUNTRY

FEELING USELESS—WAITANGI DAY
WILDERNESS—GODZONE

Once again there's no respite with this heavy, cruel cold rain, so just after sunrise I pull on my waterproofs and race relentlessly to Swannanoa, just outside Christchurch. This is where I'd collected the bike from and thought, as it was on my route today, it would be a good idea to get everything checked over by experts before another month out on the road.

And true to their word, Carole and her crew look the Bonnie over and confidently stick their thumbs up that all's well. Coincidentally, they're also prepping their own bikes to ride southbound later that day to Invercargill and invite me to a party they're organizing there later that weekend! Something about whiskey and Burt Munro!

Kim, one of the girls, chirps up, "So see you at the weekend. Remember we're now off Highway 1 here, so it'll be a lot quieter.

Just continue for literally miles and miles along the Tram Road until you can't go any further and then simply turn left onto 72. Ride safe, and hopefully this miserable weather will clear up later on."

I look up at the skies finding what I've heard hard to believe. There's no respite as I ride forever along the straight Tram Road and onto the inland road from Oxford, where I stop to fill up. And just another handful of miles I'm already looking for somewhere else to shelter. This is terrible. I'm trembling with cold, and again the rain has filtered in through my jacket lining and into my gloves, leaving my fingers numb like icicles. I'm constantly wiping my visor just to see through the downpour.

The wheels continue splashing through the puddles until, due to the freezing cold weather, I can go no further and am forced to stop outside a tiny general store in Glentunnel. I've got to get out of these drenched clothes. The two ladies behind the counter, Eileen and Susan, smile in disbelief at my dishevelled look.

With an imploring look I argue my case, "Would it be at all possible, if I buy a hot drink, to warm my hands by your radiator, take these trousers off, and stay here a bit?"

They pleasantly nod and point to a stack of boxes next to the ice-cream chest and suggest laying every sopping wet thing out there. This is ridiculous. I've hardly done any mileage, and I'm already stopping. After a third coffee in their pleasant company, their smiles start to wane, making me think I've maybe outstayed my welcome and I'm now feeling more like an accessory. So I reluctantly pull on the soaked trousers and wave goodbye. Not surprisingly, my leather gloves are heavily sodden and not even worth wearing, so I chuck them in the pannier and pull out the thin summer gloves, knowing that a bit further on they'll also be drenched and useless.

I grit my teeth and get on with the job to cover as many miles as possible through this drenched, wretched but "pretty if it was dry" landscape.

Eighty kilometres further on I can't quite believe it. The skies have finally opened up, and is that really a ray of sunshine I see? Miraculously, by the time I reach the next gas station in Mayfield, the rain has totally stopped. But I still have a problem. I'm freezing cold and sodden through like a sponge. I need to change out of these wet, useless clothes. My only choice is to park the bike next to an open garage filled with cars jacked up, and I notice a guy working underneath one.

"Excuse me. Don't worry, I'm going to fill up, but I urgently need to change out of these sodden clothes and put some dry ones on. I've just been through hell!"

The guy in blue working overalls slides his wheelie tray that he's been lying on from under the car, gets up, and wipes his hands on an oily rag. But it's his warm, welcoming smile that makes me already feel I'll be alright. "Oh my god, you look like a wet rag doll. Go up those stairs to the garage workshop where you can change. Here's a clean towel. By the way, my name's Happy!"

I pull off my boots, waterproof (ha ha!) trousers, jacket, and sodden tops and leave them strewn on the floor around the bike. Wearing just long johns and a vest, I rummage through my bag for replacement trousers and tops. By the time I've walked back to the bike, re-attired in dry clothes, the sun's come out and I see a big steak and cheese pie has been thoughtfully placed on my tank. I rip the bag open and take a very large bite. I walk over to Happy, who as his name suggests, is now smiling filling cars with petrol and speaking with a handful of local bikers also heading to Invercargill.

"Happy, I can't express how grateful I am. You've literally been my saviour and made me very happy too!"

We both smile and wave each other goodbye, but not before I've eaten the whole pie!

It's at the prosperous farming town of Geraldine, with its art galleries and gastro food stores, that I'm now feeling one hundred per cent better and turn the bike northwards onto Route 79 and further into the high Tussock grasslands and wild merino wool pastures of Mackenzie Country. And it's here that I'm treated by the sudden appearance of vast, open, undulating plains in multi-toned greens with a fringe of distant mountains out on the horizon. This is a truly diverse and beautiful place, particularly from Burkes Pass on Highway 8 at an elevation of 700 metres. I grin. I'm dry and not rain-drenched and I'm all on my own in this sparsely populated rural area riding through ever widening valleys and snow-capped landscapes on the Starlight Highway to Lake Tekapo, with at the moment, no impatient traffic pestering me.

This massive basin area was named after James McKenzie, a shepherd and sheep thief of Scottish origin who herded his stolen flocks in what was then in the mid-1800s almost empty of any human presence. McKenzie, or Jock the Outlaw, became one of New Zealand's most enduring folk heroes.

It was also the New Zealand poet Thomas Bracken who was the first person to use the phrase *God's own country* in a poem he wrote in the 1880s. People agreed that there was so much diversity in the landscape and in such a small area that the phrase was abbreviated to *Godzone* and has been used ever since.

But this tranquil heaven doesn't last long. As I approach Lake Tekapo, vehicles appear out of every direction. Every other four-wheeler is an SUV hauling a boat, with other SUVs driving at scary speeds. As I ride down one incline, I see an oncoming car dangerously overtake another vehicle at such a speed that I'm forced to brake fast and slow down just to let him get through. That's scared me, and as he passes I shake a finger to warn him to slow down, but all he does is put an aggressive two finger V-sign up at me expressing a silent "F . . . You, I don't care!" attitude. Not pleasant, but I'd also forgotten it was New Zealand's national holiday, or Waitangi Day, and everyone was in a rush to get somewhere. Boy, do I pick the best days to travel.

But all was forgiven when after 311 kilometres I reach the mesmerizing, crystal clear, aquamarine glacier-fed Lake Tekapo. At 700 metres above sea level, the region has some of the cleanest air in the Southern Hemisphere and is also one of the best places to stargaze. In fact, the pristine sky of the Mackenzie Basin is now internationally acknowledged as a Gold Status Dark Sky Reserve for spectacular views up to the southern skies. Even with just a naked eye I'd be able to see the Milky Way galaxy, the Southern Cross, and the seasonal planets. Tonight I'd convinced myself was going to be good, as the sky was now almost cloudless.

Tonight of all nights, due to the spectacle I was going to witness later on, I'd splashed out and treated myself for a stay at The Chalet overlooking Lake Tekapo and just a couple of minutes' stroll to the Church of the Good Shepherd. The little church, built in the 1930s, is a beautiful memorial to the Mackenzie Country pioneers.

With a warm welcome from Walter and Zita, my hosts, I'm led to a sumptuous room with spine chilling views over the icy blue lake, and which I already feel is worth the money, as all my wet clothes are laid out to dry on my own sunny south-facing veranda. And out in the distance I make out the tiny lakeside church. But it looks more like a termite hill, with the tiny dots of people coming in and out of it and crawling up and down its slopes on this national holiday. I'll wait a lot later to make my own pilgrimage or maybe even get up early before I leave to see the sun rising from behind it.

By late afternoon, mingling with crowds of Chinese, Japanese, and German speaking tourists, I zig-zag along the roadside ribbon of cafés and gift shops to try and find a place—any place—to get a meal after this long gruelling day on the road. Everywhere is packed. I have no other choice but to take an early slot at the Kohan Sushi Bar. And what a sight in this jam-packed room. I'm the only non-Asian person. Everyone else, I'm told by a reliable source in the kitchen, are Chinese. Again, almost everyone is crazily mesmerized looking at their cell phone screens and not directly out of the windows to the spectacular jaw-dropping views. How are the kids going to grow up knowing nothing else besides looking at the world through a plastic screen?

As the sun sets, I take a blanket down to the lake and sit down with it wrapped around my shoulders and look up in awe to the vast expanse of universe; the unadulterated view of the interminable stars and planets creeping over the sky that forms our Milky Way. It's quiet now, and I'm mesmerized by this natural spectacle as the magic has returned to this place.

With a leisurely departure after a scrumptious belly filling breakfast, I ride through the settlement of Tekapo and continue through the backbone of the country on SH8. At Lake Pukati, backed by the peaks of the Southern Alps, I pull into a parking area, where I'm granted my first sighting of the 3,754 metre high Mount Cook or as it's known by it's Maori name, Aoraki, meaning "cloud piercer." But this time, as before, this epic mountain's top half is also shrouded in cloud but bizarrely surrounded by a bright blue sky. It almost feels magical.

Ngai Tahu, the Southern Maori people, have a well-known story of the creation of the South Island and the Southern Alps. Once there was no New Zealand. The Great Sea of Kiwa rolled over the place. After Raki (the Sky Father) married Papa-tua-nuku (the Earth Mother), his children from previous unions came to inspect the new wife. Four of his sons came down in a massive ceremonial canoe and, after leaving the shores of the Earth Mother, put out to sea. But they found no land and disaster overtook them. Instead of being lifted back into the skies, their boat sank onto an undersea ridge and turned to stone. Unfortunately, it sank unevenly, with the whole canoe forming the South Island with the western side being much higher than the eastern. The four travelling sons clambered up onto the high side where they were also turned to stone. Each son became a mountain; the eldest Aoraki became Mount Cook and his three younger brothers became the three peaks nearest to him, Mount Dampier, Mount Teichelmann, and Mount Tasman. Later shaping of the land was done by several great chiefs using magic to also dig and carve out the great lakes.

I bring the engine back to life again and head on out, glancing one last time over my shoulder to the mountains surrounded by this seemingly wild, untouched land. It's interesting that this magnificent group of mountains were known to the early European settlers for many years before the Mackenzie plains were actually discovered. My final destination today is Timaru, much further down on the south coast, but it was even there that these giant mountains could be seen. Generally, it has to be said, that the early settlers there were too preoccupied with finding farming land and carving out a living to be interested in exploring the forbidding mountains to the west. But a story goes that Julius von Haast, a German born geologist and explorer while out on an expedition sketching and mapping the lower slopes of Mount Cook in 1869, had just commented to his companion that they were higher up the mountain than anyone had ever been when they were interrupted by a shout from a ridge above warning them not to disturb the sheep. The owner of nearby Birch Hill Station was already grazing his sheep there!

I sweep joyfully past the open vast plains on this bright sun-filled morning until all of a sudden I'm forced to slow down. A section of road works appears in this wilderness with the habitual "Stop" sign. There are a small line of cars already waiting, and as I pass them I stop behind three bikers: a green Norton, a Triumph Rocket 2300cc, and a racing Yamaha. Due to their diversity, I'd be a little surprised if they were travelling together, but during the Burt Munro week anything is possible. The round panel is swivelled to "Go" by one of the workmen, and the bikes shoot off, with me following on their tails through this majestic highlands country. This really is the time to twist that throttle, race, and fly forward through these perfect long stretches of roads, where our four bikes now have the road to all ourselves.

The SH8 continues to lead us through the vast expanses of tussock and sheep country, where thirty kilometres south from Twizell we all reach the junction settlement of Omarama. I ride with the bikers, with dozens more now already parked up, into the Oasis Café and fuel station.

I'm bedazzled to see such a highly decorated, hi-spec trike with matching flame-painted trailer when the guy gets off and wanders over, "Good to see a gal riding here in the Highlands. You heading to Burt's weekend too?"

I smile, "You bet you! But thought I'd soak up some of the inland scenery instead of continuing straight down on Highway 1."

"Good decision, as that road's gonna be pretty busy, and at least you'll get away from some of the trucks for a while." He waves. "See you over in Invercargill!"

It definitely looks like everyone has the same plan but just taking different routes to get there, because as I leave I'm again the only biker heading south down the 83. I'm guessing the others are probably continuing through the country on Highway 6, which will finally lead them directly into Invercargill.

And miraculously, almost immediately, the landscape changes once again. Along this quiet road the mountains start to encroach into the plains getting ever closer to the lakes until the road lazily winds in and out of them on this flat valley floor. By the time I've passed the giant Aviemore Dam and reached Kurow, on the banks of the Waitaki River, barren and fir tree dotted hills have almost reached the edges of this sleepy little roadside settlement. But there's also a feeling that I'm entering some form of civilization again. The neighbouring views along the roadside confirm this as I pass more and more cultivated lands, wheat and crop fields, cattle bunched within fenced boundaries, and traffic rushing south to the coast.

Signs for Oamaru's town centre come into view, and I'm soon riding down this pretty, relaxed-feeling town known for its Victorian architecture and penguin colonies. This place feels good, and I'm not surprised to later learn that it's one of New Zealand's most alluring and unspoilt provincial cities, with plenty of things to see to make it worth staying for a day or two.

I park the bike conveniently outside the Steampunk HQ and close to a precariously perched steam engine. This quirky museum has also made Oamaru New Zealand's steampunk capital. I tie the helmet onto the bike and take a little promenade through the historic Harbour Street and down to the harbour's dock and jetties where colonies of little blue penguins come up to nest. But that's not until dusk. Not for the first time, this is another place I would have liked to stay at longer, but the call of the South is ringing in my ears, with still almost 400 kilometres to cover by tomorrow night to reach the Island's southernmost tip.

I miss the opportunity to stock up on food, thinking fifteen kilometres further south in Kakanui there'll be all I need for my one night stop-over. But again, back on the road the distances feel misleadingly longer. I finally turn off Highway 1 and enter a picturesque country road that follows a river up to a steep hillside overlooking the sea. A few houses are dotted around to create this settlement. I park up outside a wood-stilted beach house and wander up to the front door. There's no one here except for a black and brown sheepdog wagging its tail and looking up at the letterbox that has an envelope sticking out with my name on it.

I pull it out and take out a set of keys with a note inside it: "Welcome Zoë. We hope you have a great time here. The door to your place is on the side. Our settlement has one shop over the river bridge where you might find some basics and there're also some houses that might be selling vegetables out on the road. The beach is in the opposite direction but I'm sure Colin our dog will show you around! Have fun, Jan."

Walking down the garden pathway, I enter a beautifully furnished 1960s Conran-style flatette, where I impatiently change into shorts and flip flops. With food at the forefront of my priorities, I stuff some dollar notes into my pocket and walk down the hill with Colin chasing after me. Past a small church with sheep grazing in the graveyard, along the estuary river with white herons waiting to pounce on fish, and over a narrow bridge, I walk into a small grocery shop with an old shopkeeper behind an equally old fashioned till. Colin waits outside while I pick up one onion, a pot of yoghurt, and a banana from the small, limited choice of goods. I look around, as there's something missing.

Looking over the till, I ask with a questioning look, "Excuse me, but do you by any chance sell wine?"

The apron-dressed man replies, "That'll be the room next door. Just go to that counter and I'll join you!"

That's strange. Mystified, I walk back outside onto the pavement and wander back in through another door to see only an empty darkened room with a bare counter but with some hopeful bottles of wine and cases of beer stacked behind it. The old guy magically appears again behind this counter.

"I'm sorry, but due to licensing laws we have to keep this place separate!"

On the way back along the lane's grassy verges, I pick up bags of green and yellow peppers and juicy, ripe black tomatoes without forgetting to drop a five dollar bill in the Trust Box. All this will make a fine spaghetti sauce! Colin's impatient to leave and, without asking for permission, dashes across the bridge, sniffing out maybe the scent of wild rabbits in the undergrowth. The bags of food are left at the beach house, as Colin then barks and leads me wagging his tail down another steep road to the gently lapping sea surrounded by round green hills.

Besides a few cabbage trees dotted about, this sedate coast could easily be somewhere in Britain. But it's walking down to the beach that I see enormous fields of giant seaweed that have been washed up close to the stony shoreline due to the recent storm. We both dip our feet and paws in but it's just too cold, and Colin impatiently scampers back up the beach with me following to finally relax back on the hill.

13

THROUGH THE CAITLINS

TARTAN & BAGPIPES—LITTLE WALES
A LOST GYPSY—GREAZY DOGS

With Colin wagging his tail "goodbye," the bike impatiently roars back and we're off for another unknown set of adventures. Finally heading for Invercargill, the day's looking perfect, with not a single cloud in the early morning bluest of blue skies, as I settle in the seat and ride through tiny, lost country lanes. The aim's to go along these for as long as possible before being forced to get back onto the main highway.

And I'm not disappointed. As the sun creeps up, the long black shadow of me and the bike spreads out across the fields. The roads aren't even on my map, and I just continue to meander alongside the bountiful gold wheat fields, where combine harvesters out in the distance are starting to create tapestry designs through the landscape. And just as close, on my other side of the aptly named Beach Road, is the sea with white cylindrical waves crashing onto the massive expanses of untamed beaches. This continues for twenty perfect kilometres, and these are, in my mind, some of the most beautiful landscapes I've ridden through in New Zealand.

Tiny Waianakarua Road leads me alongside its namesake river, over some bumpy railway tracks, and all of sudden back to reality onto Highway 1. But I'm already starting to see that these pretty, straight coastal roads are gradually getting quieter. And it's not before long and no more than ten kilometres that I've turned off towards another remote beach to witness the phenomena of the Moeraki Boulders. I park up in an empty lot near the beach, kick off my boots, and squeeze barefooted through a hedge down the sandy slope onto a soft, sandy beach where the sea is receding outwards. No one is here except for me and hundreds of strange giant grey spherical rock boulders that lie partially submerged on the tide line, looking like they're somehow rolling out into the distance. Some are broken, revealing the beautiful honeycomb centres, and it's truly a sight I'd never seen before and one I don't think I'll see again anywhere else.

As the wild kilometres are being killed and eaten up, so the countryside is once again changing. About a hundred kilometres from the early Scottish settlement of Dunedin, mountains are starting to appear again, but this time it's very different. They're covered in green and gold bracken; fir trees and lakes are dotted around them, which make this place look unbelievably like the real

Scottish Highlands. I almost feel like rubbing my eyes in disbelief at how incredibly authentic it all looks. I'm almost imagining I'll soon be seeing kilt-clad hitchhikers!

Unsurprisingly, nature's soon calling, and I need to find a place to stop and, you could say, lighten the load! As I'd already experienced with the traffic, it was difficult to just pull up, and sometimes the incline on the sides of the roads were too steep to safely park the heavy bike without my permanent fear of it falling over into the ditch. No, I'll go on a bit further, as I see a timely sign for the settlement of Waitati. Blueskin Nurseries beckons me in, and three wonderful apron-clad people; Callum, Maxwell, and Jess; direct me to the "little room" and then to a mouth-watering gastro display of food on the café's counter. I pack the tank bag full with massive blueberry and cinnamon muffins, a chocolate and coconut lamington, a salmon filo pastry, and a couple of spinach and cheese puffs. These will all do nicely for, let's see . . . lunch, more stops, emergency back-ups, feeding hungry sheep . . . well that's my excuse as I drink a coffee in the ornate garden and reflect that this spontaneous stop was, indeed, a very successful mission.

The phone suddenly vibrates with a message: "Hi it's Rachel from Pakiri. Believe me, I'm still trying to help you get to Paradise! But the horse outfit said they don't go that far and are already booked. Maybe you can find someone in Glenorchy with a truck to get you there. Good luck! x"

I ruminate on what I've just read, which ironically makes me even more adamant that I'm going to find my Paradise! It surely can't be that difficult. Maybe she's right and I need to wait until I get to this back of beyond place of Glenorchy to suss the joint and see who I can coerce to take me.

It's surprisingly still early, and as I'm only twenty-five kilometres away from Dunedin, the large student town with the world's steepest street, I decide to make a slight detour and go take a cheeky look. Dunedin Railway Station, in Anzac Square, is where I park up first, which is pretty difficult to miss due to its ornate Victorian towers and decorative colourful flower gardens around it. And still not a person in sight. I once again kick the bike into life and pull up next in the town's central plaza, The Octagon, in front of Saint Paul's Cathedral and next to Robert Burns. This was the first public sculpture created in 1887 and symbolic of Dunedin's Scottish origins.

The New Zealand Company selected the Otago Harbour for a Scottish settlement as early as 1840 and purchased land from the local Maori, but it wasn't until eight years later that the first migrant ships arrived, on board of which was the Reverend Thomas Burns. He was the nephew of Richard Burns, the Scottish poet who wrote the masterpiece *Auld Lang Syne*, for whose birthday Scots around the world still celebrate with a Burns Supper of haggis, whiskey, and poem recitals on the 25th of January. And fast forward to 1861, Australian prospectors discover gold nearby and a gold rush is created, expanding the city to briefly become New Zealand's largest and which helps finance some of its beautiful architecture. Things over time gradually declined, but New Zealand's largest gold mining operation is still located only about an hour north of the city.

Only a bit further on at Balcutha, I turn off onto the much less-travelled Highway 92, which would lick the southernmost parts of the Caitlins Coastline, finally taking me into Invercargill. Green patchwork fields are sewn together through the quiet wild countryside, with beautiful curving smooth roads cutting through them. Wild clumps of the creamy, white pampas grasses, New Zealand's largest native grass, blow softly back and forth on the day's warm breeze. This is sheer joy.

Passing Owaka, the only settlement of any size within the Caitlins and little more than a farming settlement crossroads, I ride alongside the Caitlins Lake and stop on the other side of the bridge to take a better look around me. The large, heavy cumulus clouds are mirrored in the water, with the sun bouncing off the rounded hills making this a perfect day for biking and so much warmer than I'd expected travelling so far south.

I continue on, but it's now, almost for the first time, that I'm seeing motorcycles starting to pass me and wave out to me from every direction. Some are without any luggage, so maybe out on a daytrip from Invercargill, while others riding in my direction are heavily loaded, which only means one thing. We're going to spend an adrenaline-filled four days at the famous Burt Munro Challenge Races. But I've maybe jumped the gun here in not already explaining the significance of this event, who Burt Munro is, and why Invercargill is the country's motorcycle racing mecca.

Born in Edendale, New Zealand, in 1899, Burt Munro's dedication to motorcycles was enormous and his life achievements legendary. He bought his first Indian Scout in 1920 for £100, with a top speed of fifty miles per hour, but which he would continue to modify and customize for the rest of his life. Just six years later he races the Indian for the first time, by 1930 it's capable of ninety miles per hour, and by 1937 it's called the Munro Special and is capable of speeds up to 110 mph. After setting a number of New Zealand land speed records in the 1940s and '50s his next goal was to race at the legendary Bonneville Salt Flats in America. Burt was sixty-three when he first competed, and in 1962 set a land speed record on his bike of 178.97mph. He set two more world records there in 1967 of 183.58 mph, which still stands today, and on this trip also managed to hit 190.07 mph during qualifications, being the fastest ever recorded on an Indian motorcycle. Following the success of the *World's Fastest Indian* film starring Anthony Hopkins, the Southland Motorcycle Club created the annual "Burt Munro Challenge," with the first event in 2006 to honour his ingenuity and love of speed. Even Guy Martin, our UK racing hero and mechanic, had come to race here in 2016. The event represents speedway, drag, and street racing, a hill climb, and beach racing at Oreti Beach, where Burt had spent years modifying and testing his bike out on these long stretches of sand.

Thousands upon thousands of people are expected to turn up for this four-day extravaganza, changing a normally quiet nondescript far-away place to the most exciting and diverse racing spectacle in the southern hemisphere.

The remote, sub-tropical Papatowai Highway finally brings me to the very top of a spectacular green mountainous valley stretching out forever. I just have to stop and walk to the edge to breathe in the unbelievable beauty of this extraordinary view. With perfect sunny skies, it looks like a drug-induced version of the Brecon Beacons, the Snowdonia National Park, the Elan Valley, and the Black Mountains of Wales all rolled into one. There aren't many times I'm speechless, but this is one of them and words just can't do it justice. You'll just have to believe me!

I get back on to leave, but there's already a problem. Just a few metres ahead at the ridge of this hill I see three orange road cones strangely placed right across it. There are no signs, no explanation, and nobody around to give any instructions. In any other normal situation this would mean strictly no entrance. But this wasn't normal. I weigh up the situation. I was too far to reasonably double-track back all the way to Highway 1. There were no other roads. But thinking rationally, there had been quite a few bikers who had passed me, and they must have continued riding up and through this same road. I'm going to take a gamble.

I carefully ride through the cones and look ahead that maybe the road hasn't disappeared down the hillside! Everything looks perfect, so I twist the throttle, kick the gears up, and continue to head off through this wild land. By the time I've crossed the Tahakopa River into the tiny place of Papatowai, I'm dying for a drink and hungrily wanting to indulge in some of the sustenance I'd crammed into my tank bag from the garden centre. I park outside an old bus beside the main road, otherwise known in these parts as the Lost Gypsy Gallery, which contains bizarre recycled materials that have become strangely animated.

I wander past a metal letterbox in the shape of a massive whale with a Barbie doll riding it and a dog's skeleton peddling an old bicycle and head to a little corrugated cabin serving coffee. Next to it a guy in a flowery blue shirt is loudly hammering to death some sort of inanimate junk. This is Blair Somerville, the creator of this crazy wonderland.

"What a treasure trove of wackiness. It's brilliant what you've made, but why do you do it?"

He smiles, wiping the sweat from his forehead, and provides a simple but perfect reply, "'Cos there's nothing better to do!"

343 kilometres further south from where I set off this morning, I enter the long, wide streets of Invercargill and pull up in a little residential cul-de-sac, where I'll be laying my head for the next four nights. As promised, Laura, my host, has kindly left the front door key under the mat.

And on my bed lies the set of six colourful race tickets, which I'd got posted here. Unfortunately, I hadn't arrived in time for the classic motorcycle hill climb that had taken place earlier in the morning, but no doubt, I'd probably hear about it from someone later on. Right now all I need do is pull everything off the bike, splash my face clean, and ride out to Teretonga Park for the twilight drag racing event. Crossing a little bridge, I'm soon heading out along flat country roads until I pull up in a grassy parking area, also within walking distance of the rally site where most people are camping and where I plan to visit tomorrow. A few people look the bike over, including a tall head-shaved guy wearing a leather club jacket embellished with the Greazy Dogs MC symbols.

Almost immediately, this feels like a pretty laid-back place, with bikes and trucks crammed up next to each other in rows facing the quarter-mile track. It also looks like there's a general bike show going on in the parking area, as all the two-wheels are looking very shiny. I wander up and down to find a suitable place to lie on the grass to watch the races. An old chap is sitting on his own at the front with a picnic basket. I amble over, and he kindly puts his hand out, offering me space next to him to plonk me and my stuff down.

"Thanks so much. That's really kind. Do you mind terribly keeping an eye on my jacket and helmet, so I can take a little walk around before the racing starts?"

"For sure! Take your time. I'll make an effort to keep your space. This is a new event this year that replaced the Moto Cross, which still keeps its dates in November. So this should be interesting."

I walk in and out of the crowds and see a large group of bikes with some guys and a few policemen having a friendly chat. They are all proudly showing their Greazy Dogs MC badges. Bizarrely, the same shaven-head guy notices me, smiles, and with his two fingers shows me the devils sign. What else can I do but approach, knowing I'm not risking too much because of the smiling coppers next to them. And with that, he inquisitively walks over with two other club members.

"Good to see a chick riding. Where have you come from?"

"Came in from the North Island just a few days ago."

"Yea, we're the North Island bike club chapter from the Auckland area. We're down here specially just for the races."

And with that we shake hands, and the Greazy Dogs line up for a photo, throwing their arms around each other.

I then cheekily ask if they could maybe turn around so I can also take a picture of their symbolic growling dog with wings patch on their jacket backs.

One of them replies smiling, "Only if you turn and shake your ass for us first!"

I wander back to the drag strip and sit next to my new friend Bill, the old guy who'd saved me a spot.

"Good to see you again. The racing's just gonna start. Would you like a cup of tea?"

I smile, "For sure! That would do nicely!"

Filling the little cup and passing it to me he adds, "So I guess this must be your first time, that is, hearing your accent?"

"Yes, I've waited a long time to experience this and to understand why everybody loves Burt Munro."

"Well you're going to see some stuff here tonight. It's open for riders to enter on competition bikes or just what you rode to the event on!"

I sit back against my jacket and relax sipping the warm, sweet tea.

"Let me tell you a story that's true. My uncle, Frank Dahlenbergh, used to have an Indian with a sidecar and would ride along with Burt Munro. They were just young jokers back in the '40s!"

I nod, holding the warm cup between my hands, and just let him continue talking. "Yes, those were the days. But I also had a lot of fun this morning joining a great crowd for the hill climb. It's held each year on the bumpy, steep, and exciting ribbon of tarmac that goes all the way from Bluff to the summit. You should bike over there, as it's also New Zealand's earliest colonial settlement and where you can get your photo taken next to the place marking it as the country's most southerly point. And at the top of the summit, where I was, there are brilliant views over the aluminium smelter and Stewart Island. The racing was good too—noisy and exciting. We also had the first appearance of those intrepid Aussies, the crew from across the ditch, and their hand-change, girder-forked Indians and Harleys. And they'll be doing the other races. But the quickest rider was Mitch Rees, who managed to squeeze his brother, Damon, into second spot.

We and the thousands of others clap and applaud throughout the evening until it's time to leave. If tonight's anything to go by, then I'm in for a hell of a weekend.

14

Offerings to the God of Speed

*"You can live more in five minutes on a motorcycle in some of
these events I've been in than some people do in a lifetime!"*
Burt Munro

Suddenly, the cat makes a deliberate kamikaze jump from the
wall, spilling the coffee over the terrace table and drenching my
precious festival race tickets. I flap them desperately in the air to dry
and believe this is maybe a sign to shift and get to know Invercargill
a little better before the day disappears and the beach races start in
the afternoon.

But before I even get up, my phone buzzes with a message: "Hi.
This is Kim from Pacific Motorcycles. We got in last night. We'd
love you to come and join us for a party tonight at the Transport
World on Tay Street. There'll be a charity auction for the special
"Spirit of Munro" whiskey and Burt's son, John Munro, will be
appearing. We'll introduce you. See ya there!"

I smile at this unexpected news and make a mental note. Leaving
the empty house, as Laura had already left for work at Invercargill's
Flight Centre, I jump onto my unusually unloaded bike to go
a-wandering. A couple of miles further, heading back towards

Teretonga Park where I'd been last night, I roll into the rally site to pick up my event pass and lanyard and obligatory souvenir T-shirt. The site is ridiculously well appointed, with pop-up restaurants, shops, and music stages, for the 3,000 inhabitants who are going to make it their Southlands temporary party home. Well it's almost perfect until I walk to the fleet of portaloos and curiously read a sign: "SHOWERS—LADIES ONLY BETWEEN 8.00—9.00AM." I gasp, thinking that's pretty strict for the gals staying here.

An arm-tattooed guy with a towel wrapped around his waist approaches me looking at the sign and jokingly blurts out, "Yep, that's the only time to wash your crevices! But for sure you can shower with the guys any other time, but you'll have to wear your undies."

I swallow at his direct remark but giggle politely as I walk away. The bike bumps out over the grassy rally site, and I head back into town onto the main thoroughfare of Dee Street, where hundreds of bikers are starting to cruise up and down, with some squeezing in between rows of other bikes now lining the walkways. Just as I've found a spot, luckily outside Hayes & Son hardware store, and I'm carefully reversing into it, a guy on an Enfield passes, frantically waving to me and turning back up the street towards me. I can't believe who I'm seeing. It's Nich, a guy I know from the biking circuit back in the UK and who'd just shipped his Enfield over to tour New Zealand and Australia for a handful of months.

"Jeez, Nich, what a coincidence and what a small world! So you and the bike got here OK?"

He pulls his visor up to speak, "Boy, don't start me. It got held up at customs in Auckland, so I'm a couple of weeks behind schedule, but I wasn't going to miss this place for the world! I haven't even had breakfast yet. Do you want to grab a coffee?"

"For sure! I'm also invited to a whiskey party tonight. You should come along. It should be interesting, as Burt's son may be there."

We grab a table on the pavement, and Nich browses the Tahuatara Café's menu and catches the eye of the waitress. "That sounds like a great idea. Count me in. I could pick you up from your place, so you can have a dram or two," and looking at the aproned girl adds, "and yes please, I'll have your Southland Sushi!"

A few moments later the sushi arrives; a slice of processed cheese on a slice of white bread. I'm not impressed, but Nich smiles at it looking like he hasn't eaten in a while. So the plan's set to meet up later for Burt's drinks, while before that, we'll both go our own ways to further soak up this place. As we stroll back to the bikes, the temptation and curiosity's too great, so we wander into the E. Hayes & Sons hardware store. Amongst all the aisles, together with the spanners, hedge trimmers, and paint, is the crazy collection of classic cars and historic motorcycles. But the star attraction is the record breaking 1920 600cc Indian Scout ridden by Burt Munro.

By 1975 Burt makes one last trip to Bonneville, and then seventy-six years old, is told by race officials he's too old to race. Just two years later, he has a stroke and sells the Munro Special Indian to his friends, Norman and Neville Hayes, who own the store. All of Burt's "Offerings to the God of Speed" motorcycle parts are also displayed here in glass-fronted wood cabinets. And just a year later, on 6 January 1978, he passes away.

Walking out of the hardware store, I wave Nich goodbye and walk over to Queen's Park and the pyramid-shaped Southland Museum and Art Gallery. It's here I'm indulged in learning more about New Zealand's tiny clusters of sub-Antarctic islands, and the sealers who survived there, lying between New Zealand and Antarctica. I also curiously learn more about the Polynesian Panthers who stood up for the Pacific communities living in New Zealand. Back in the 1960s these people had arrived believing there'd be better job opportunities to make money, much more than back home, and save towards building homes back on their islands. They also believed the education given to their children would be the key to their success, but most only landed dirty jobs cleaning factories, hospitals, and the streets. The lifestyle was totally different, with much resistance in being able to get included in society. So in 1971 the Polynesian Panther Party, a revolutionary resistance movement, was created to carry on the fight against xenophobia and oppression.

I walk out into the sunshine and see Burt is again not far away, as a replica statue of him and the Indian is standing in a prime spot outside the museum with fresh red roses scattered over it! Walking back to the bike on the main thoroughfare I pass another statue. But this beautiful, much older stone one, in honour of the Southland servicemen and women who lost their lives in the First and Second World Wars, seems awkwardly out of place and somehow lost its importance outside the cheap consumer world of McDonalds.

I squeeze out from between two bikes and head out of town. The road from Invercargill to the hallowed sands of Oreti Beach literally finishes through the dunes onto the broad expanse of sand, where like most of the others, I park up among the hundreds of other spectators' bikes. I'm close to two stunning red and orange

1950s Indian Chief Roadmasters, with their black tasseled leather side bags and old white enamel and silver Indian heads on the fenders, attracting an embarrassing number of admiring onlookers.

A fluorescent marshal approaches me pointing to my bike, "Make sure to wedge something under the foot stand so it doesn't sink. It's getting crazy here. It's been sold out before the practice even started, and we've stopped counting after 3,000 folk passed through the gates. There must be over a thousand bikes, from classics to racers, and that shuttle service is going hard-out from the rally site as well. Have a good one. Head up into the high sand dunes for a better view of the circuit."

So I clamber on my knees and hands up a dune and, shielded from the light wind, nestle into the sand, looking out to the track with the sea behind it. With sprint races for all classes, it was like peeling back time, as the machines—many almost too pretty to be thrashed on the beach (nah, not really)—with the sounds and smells of decades past were appreciated by the clapping crowds. The pits, with their trucks and bikes, were a mix of all ages, both road and dirt and simply just shoulder to shoulder supporting each other's racing. One of the classic road bikes was putting up a fight to cough into life, and it was a couple of young, fit moto lads that provided the necessary push to get it away along the sand.

And when the young guns on their motos let loose on the half-mile hardened sand straights, backing their machines in from way out, probably almost from Fiordland, it was truly exciting. The major race was won by the Australian Damien Koppe, which meant the coveted trophy was heading across the ditch for the first time, with raucous loud cheers from the supporters. The tide was turning as we all started to head back across the beach to find our bikes and get ready for the evening ahead.

A lot later that night, Nich picks me up and we ride back into town on his Enfield. The party's already in full swing as we walk towards the bar, where somebody pats me on the back. It's Matt, one of the guys from the New Zealand Whiskey Collection, organizing the evening and who I'd met a few days ago when I was getting the bike checked over outside Christchurch.

Recognising me he walks over. "Hi Zoë. Glad you could make it. The drinks are on us and enjoy the evening. A little bird told me that John Munro's arriving later to assist with the auction of our special bottle of whiskey in Burt's honour. We'll have to get you introduced."

True to his word, a short while later a white bearded guy in his 70s walks over to me with Kim. Putting his hand out to shake mine he smiles, "Welcome to Invercargill. Let's see what we can rustle up."

And with that, John Munro and I both walk over to an old Indian that he spontaneously gets on and beckons me over to sit behind as his pillion. This is a blast! While dozens of people are taking photos of him, he looks over his shoulder to me, "You know, my father's always with us. Only last year in 2017 I was at the Bonneville Salt Flats and I met this guy. He told me that Burt had inspired him so much that seven years ago he buys a bike and learns to ride, and then that very year I meet him he goes on to beat an AMA land speed record! That's pretty unbelievable, yea?"

With that he's grabbed by some other person and disappears into the crowds.

Not too early, but early enough, the next morning I'm breezing further south through the ever increasing desolate, flatlands to Bluff. As I arrive at this old fishing town, settled in 1824, I can see it's starting to look a bit rough around the edges. Battered and boarded up old wooden framed and corrugated roof homes forlornly overlook the industrial South Port and two giant white fuel tank containers. Even the one solitary café is sadly closed. But I'm here to go just that wee bit further, a total of twenty-nine kilometres south from Invercargill, to reach Stirling Point, where State Highway 1 finally ends. A couple of other bikers are also overlooking the wild coastal shoreline and getting their photo taken next to the yellow multi-armed signpost that marks the distance to major places around the world: London 18,958 kms, Sydney 2,000 kms, New York 15,008 kms, Cape Reinga 1,401 kms.

I leave the bike and walk over to hug and kiss the post, now knowing I've completed, since also embracing the sister post in Cape Reinga at the tip of the North Island, the entire length of New Zealand. I look at my watch and remember promising to get back to the Classic Motorcycle Mecca on Tay Street. At the party last night, I'd met Dave Roberts, who's the Mecca's Collections Manager, and he'd kindly invited me back to personally show me around. I'd been most flattered so didn't want to be late.

Returning to Invercargill, I notice a line of bike dealerships, including Triumph, which has a large banner proudly boasting it to be the world's most southern dealer. On this Saturday morning they certainly look like they're doing some business, with the punters sitting excitedly on the new bikes and walking out with bags of goodies.

I park up in Tay Street and wander back into the museum, where Dave gives me a smiling welcome, "Hey Zoë, glad you could make it and hope you've recovered from last night. I've only got half an hour or so but thought you'd appreciate a quick walk around with me."

I'm surprised by his generosity and gladly nod. This place, even for those not interested in two wheels, is beautiful, with hundreds of bikes gracefully displayed on shining wooden floors.

"We've got the largest display of classic motorcycles in the country. This collection, formerly known as New Zealand Classic Motorcycles, used to be housed in Nelson before the entire collection was sold to Transport World in 2016, who also owns the big Transport World Museum up the street. They built this brand new place to house over 300 incredible bikes and brilliant original artwork and posters. We've got so much mouth-licking collectable stuff, from a 1902 Peugeot up to a Simms Corbin Custom. And we have loads of stories in how the founder collected them."

"Yes, believe it not, this all used to be one man's collection, Tom Sturgess, who they say bought all the bikes with his heart rather than his head. You're not going to see anything like this in the southern hemisphere. I have a great personal story of how probably our most prized possession was sourced. It's the British 1931 AJS S-3, where only ten were ever produced. Unfortunately, this model contributed to AJS's demise, as it was too innovative and expensive for people in the Great Depression with an original value of $200. However, all that said, it was purchased new in Blenheim but left in a shed until the '50s. Somehow, it was again found in another shed over in the US in 1962 and finally sold to Tom at a Bonhams auction in Las Vegas. But little did Tom realize that the bike had originally come from a guy from his own town of Nelson, and coincidentally, my parents lived next door to the owner, often seeing back in those days the same bike being wheeled out of the garage! As we have the bike's total provenance, it's now worth about $50,000! Funny how things come full circle."

Looking up at the large wall clock, Dave sighs. "Hey I gotta go, but enjoy your stay in Invercargill and ride safe wherever that roads take you!"

I also glance at my watch. "Me too. I'm riding over to Oreti Park now for the Speedway Races."

In less than fifteen minutes I've parked up in a massive newly mown field full of vehicles next to the racetrack. And as I enter through the gates. there are already thousands of other enthusiastic spectators packed around the key vantage points with their picnics and beers, ready to party. I see bikers opening up their crammed side bags and taking out armfuls of bottles of beer to join the fun, big trucks turned into corporate hospitality serving limitless drinks to their guests and families simply chilling out on this sunny afternoon. This place is heaving with what look like more people than square metres to fit into, so guys are even placing chairs up on their van roofs to get a better view over the massive oval sandy racetrack.

I literally squeeze through a hoard of people, miraculously find a spot right on one of the corners close to the fence and naively sit down, not realizing that I'd later be covered and painfully shot by gritty sand from the bikes speeding past. Next to me an older lady is sitting on a rug with her grandson, drinking tea from her flask and spooning jam onto scones.

She looks over and smiles. "It's gonna be a good afternoon. We're in for a treat. My youngest grandson is a Pee Wee."

I look back mystified and she continues, understanding my questioning look, "Oh that's our youngest kids racing. The five to six-year-olds are called Pee Wees. You've got to start them young. If you look over the track in the middle there's a smaller track, and that's where they race with starter tape, marshals waving flags, and everything to make it totally authentic."

A guy on my other side with a beer in his hand nods, "Yea, it's gonna be good if the races from the Teretonga Circuit this morning were anything to go by. There sure are a lot of people here today."

Then the races begin, with first a display from all the competitors, including the children, riding a couple of slow circuits together. I was curious to see letters and numbers on the side of every sidecar.

The friendly guy on my left takes another swig from his bottle, "Yea for sure. It's to tell you which towns they come from. Look over there. 7I is Invercargill, 8C is Christchurch, and 31D is Dunedin. We've got the first girl race team here today too. This circuit is doing good now. About thirty years ago we used to race cars on it too, but that ruined the track. Then it closed for more than ten years and finally re-opened for bikes fifteen years ago, and we haven't looked back!"

And with that, the competitions start with the sand being kicked up onto us every time the bikes race round the corner. One of the best things about the whole event, right through the classes, was the races within races in the big fields. The side cars were suicidal, with the rider racing mercilessly round the bends and the passenger, or "Swinger," leaning over so much that they were being brushed by the sand.

"I can't believe what I'm seeing. They're lunatics and getting so close to each other."

The guy, totally enraptured, quickly nods, "Yea, particularly when you know that they've got superbike engines, no brakes are fitted, and they're only permitted to change into a higher gear once the race has started. The bikes are made to turn right only, and so the swinger sits behind the rider to give traction to the rear wheel on straights then "swings" out to their right and forward to keep the bike sitting flat and to give more traction to the front wheel in corners, allowing the rear wheel to slide through the corner. It's so crazy out there that some new riders will start way back, maybe thirty metres from the starting tapes, until the officials are satisfied they're able to enter the full competition. It sure is dangerous, but the officials are also fair. If a rider damages their bike and it's a write off whilst avoiding an accident, they can use another bike in a re-started race."

My neighbour's now on a roll, and it's nice to feel I'm being given free education on this sort of racing, "But it's all a bit different with the Solo Speedway motorcycles. These are all purpose-built 500cc four-stroke methanol-powered machines. Again, take a look, they've got no brakes, with a fixed speed, as there's no gearbox which keeps the weight down. And OK yea, these ones are made to turn left only! The right hand turns are difficult, as the right foot rest is only thirty milimetres above the ground, so the bike really can't 'lay' into a right turn. So there you go, the lesson of the day—enjoy!"

It really is frantic as me and the grandmother shield our eyes and get plastered in sand. The main solo class goes down to the wire to find the winner—Ryan Terry-Daley. I am thinking I'll definitely try and check out a top-flight speedway meet when I get back home.

Early the next morning, excitement is brewing up inside me again, as it is another experience I'd never seen or done before. The Street Races are poised to be the perfect finale on this crazy weekend. As it is within easy walking distance from where I am staying, I am going to make sure to get there with plenty of time ahead of the races, to soak up the pre-race atmosphere and try and get a prime spot. Although there was a forecast for a light band of rain to come in later, it all looks good.

As I stroll to the entrance gate and show my blue ticket, I start talking with the bike builder, Lindsay Pinckerton, who had unfortunately broken down on the circuit yesterday. As we walk through to the cordoned off streets, I am beginning to realize that everyone here knows everybody else, as before long I'm introduced to Kevin, who will change my day for the better! He's the official photographer but part of the organising committee for the event and also previously an editor for one of the biking magazines here.

He courteously shakes my hand, "Zoë, great to see you. Welcome. I'm glad you're here to get some stories. Walk over to the organizers' truck with me, and I'll get you an orange "road racing official" SMCC stewards vest to wear! With that you'll be seen as a staff person, so you can go anywhere on and off-limits for the public around the track, over the tracks, and up into the viewing building. Let's also go and see a few of the guys setting up before the races."

I swallow hard. I really can't believe my luck, as now attired in a bright orange vest, we walk up into the cordoned-off back streets and through the lines of vans with the competitors' bikes parked under their awnings being prepped for the races. It's amusing, as almost immediately wearing the vest, people start coming up to me to ask questions like "Where's the coffee shack?" and "When do the races start?" I giggle, not really knowing the answers.

It looks like everyone in the New Zealand racing family is here working on their bikes and exchanging stories with their fellow racers on this early morning. Kevin walks over to the country's famous racer, Vince Burrell, and his Moto Guzzi, slapping him on the shoulder wishing him good luck. At this point, Kevin shouts into his walkie-talkie and dashes off, waving me goodbye.

As I wander down the street, I'm fascinated to witness the workings of this massive turnout. Halfway down I stop to see two very interesting looking guys working away on their bikes. This has to be worth a conversation. Both are covered in oil and grease with long hair, beards, and moustaches, looking like the epitome of the local racing scene down here in the south. We shake hands.

Nev only has one eye, covered with a patch, but knows all the local bikers and talks with an unbelievable openness about his life, "I know them all 'cos I've been around a fair bit. I've done everything from scrap metal, working on the rigs, mines, done my time in prison, sheep stations. You name it. But it's the bikes we love."

Nev slaps the other guy on the back "Ain't that right, Animal?"

This incredible looking other guy, who's name really is Animal— with old, torn and weathered leathers and a face covered in silvery stranded brown hair and a few missing teeth—seriously nods, "You bet. I don't have much budget either and live in a backyard. I've got four homemade bike frames but only one engine. So for each different event, like the beach and track, I transfer the engine onto the corresponding frame."

But they both look incredibly happy and content with life as Animal continues, "But it's good here at the races. You get to rub shoulders with everyone. See that guy over there? I'll introduce you.

Now he's famous but a great guy. It's our friend, Bill Swallow, the British classic TT racer."

And with that, we wander over to Bill, who's already in his black racing leathers and with a friendly smile beckoning us over to have a chin-wag and see his black Eldee Velocette.

Left once again to my own devices, I stroll over to the track to find a spot. But the orange jacket is still attracting a lot of attention and questions I can't answer. So finally, not wanting to embarrass the organizers, I discreetly take it off, but not before bumping into Nich, who's just arrived.

The qualifying goes like clockwork on the wide grippy surface. And with just a splattering of light rain, the racing gets under way around the streets. And then disaster strikes with a classic motorcycle leaving three distinct oil trails on different lines on ninety-five per cent of the circuit, in and out of every twist and turn; there's simply no line left to brake for the corners—and that's if you even get there. With this street racing not having the luxury of run-off and kitty-litter, any mistakes result in sudden stops, so the call is made, and sadly the racing has to be cancelled. As Nich and I walk back to the truck to hand back the jacket, we bump into Kevin.

"So sad for you that the races had to be cancelled. But it has been an amazing experience and thanks so much for the Invercargill welcome!"

He sighs, "Yes, it's really sad, as the team had spent fifteen months organizing it. We had to pull the pin to avoid any crash or multiple crashes. Our hands were tied and we're gutted but know it's the right call."

We all nod in agreement and feel that everyone must be proud of the team in their difficult decision.

It's now starting to rain, and with the crowds Nich and I walk away towards his bike. "Zoë, you fancy a Sunday morning fry up in a warm café up on the main strip?"

"For sure. I couldn't think of a better thing to do."

So with that, the Royal Enfield's started up, I pull on my baseball cap, and jump onto the back. As I hang on and we ride through the rain sodden streets, I remember what people have been saying all weekend about the Burt Munro Challenge. Although I'd only been to this one, everyone is agreeing it was definitely the best they've attended. with the biggest most enthusiastic crowds ever. For just ninety-nine dollars to spectate all six events over the four days, it was definitely worth it.

The weekend really was testament to the Invercargill community, and in particular that core bunch who made such a diverse and massive event even possible. The local council help; they even had the mayor, Tim Shadbolt, swing the starting flags on the beach.

With the world-class motorcycle attractions now in Invercargill, it makes you wonder . . . is there anywhere else that this would even be possible, let alone actual?

15

Shadowland

Fiordland Journeys—Milford Sound
Doubtful Sound—Kepler Track

The battered map with the hand drawn yellow line representing today's chosen route is staring up at me from the tank as I turn the key and accelerate out of Invercargill. There were a number of alternative roads I could have chosen today, but I'd decided on the lesser ridden Highway 99, or better known in these parts as the "Southern Scenic Route". This follows the coastline westwards for a while before finally turning northwards up to Te Anau, the gateway to Fiordland. This would cover roughly 200 kilometres, and with a cloudless day I'm praying the rain will stay away. This is exciting stuff, knowing I am finally going to witness some of the greatest wonders of the world.

The bike purrs contentedly after I've filled its tank, and I pat it encouragingly to take me out onto the quiet country road to lap up the first sunny rays of the day. This is already feeling like a good ride with very little traffic on this increasingly remote and isolated route. And very soon I've pulled up next to a little steam train engine in Riverton overlooking the old port. In its peak this little settlement had schooners arrive from Australia loaded with supplies, agricultural goods, and many immigrants. But like a lot of places here, due to falling trade, by the end of the 1800s the Customs Warehousing Port had closed and was superseded by a Fisherman's Co-operative.

My journey continues through beautiful fertile pasturelands filled with happy, grazing sheep and dotted here and there by the now familiar cabbage tree—just to remind me we're still in the sub-tropics. What a wonderful thing to be doing on a Monday morning! And it's warm, which is another surprise I wasn't expecting this far south. I'd thought it would be freezing cold, but far from it!

After a while, I leave the great stretch of almost empty scenic coastal road and start to head inland, directly northwards. Almost immediately a giant smiling sausage greets me from a massive billboard! For some unknown reason, Tuatapere is New Zealand's sausage capital, but also being the most south westerly town, it is the last place to see the sun set. Maybe then a good place for year round BBQs and hotdogs!

My curiosity continues as shortly afterwards I turn off and ride down a little nondescript bumpy track and stop in front of a beautiful old steel and hardwood bridge. This is Clifden Suspension Bridge, built in 1899 over the Waiau River and one of the longest in the South Island. I leave the bike next to a couple of campervans and wander over to this piece of history. I'm reminded of the close similarity in name and build to that of the Clifton Suspension Bridge, which was built just thirty-five years earlier and spans the Avon Gorge close to Bristol in Northern Somerset. Peering over, hundreds of sheep have walked down the quiet river banks to drink some water. Before its construction, Clifden settlers were heavily reliant on the Waiau Ferry to get their goods and stock across this once dangerous stretch of water. Though it was originally intended for horse-drawn traffic, it wasn't long before traction engines towing trailers of lime and wood became a common sight.

The pastoral charm of the Southern Scenic Route continues, where the only traffic hazards I can see would be escaping sheep running out onto the roads. But once again, even here there are sporadic logger trucks coming through from the more northerly deforested areas, not making me feel totally comfortable or safe to stop on the roadside here to take the odd spontaneous snap.

Once again, the mountains reaching far out into the distance are getting ever nearer, and reaching the T-junction on Weir Road, I turn onto Hillside Manapouri Road. It's also here that the wind re-appears, starting to harshly blow through the hills until I reach Manapouri Lake, which I'll come back to over the next few days. It's now just an easy fifteen minute ride to my base at Te Anau, the gateway town to Fiordland (yes, the spelling's correct!). As I approach the town stretches out along the pebbly shores of Lake Te Anau itself, one of New Zealand's deepest and most impressive lakes, and with yet more giant mountains standing directly behind it.

Without much hassle, I find Mokonui Street and finally park up in front of the Te Anau Youth Hostel, where handfuls of backpackers and trekkers are coming in and out. Due to its central location and where I need to get to, this will be a perfect place to stay. Again, I'm glad I'd planned things and booked everything in advance during this busier than expected season. Walking through a lounge area, once again filled with people only looking down at their phones, I'm led to a single room, relieved I won't be sharing it with snoring bunkbed companions.

Without a doubt, this is one place I'd done an extensive amount of research on, as I really wanted to get to the remoter places and experience this incredible UNESCO World Heritage Site. Also known as Te Wahipounamu, or the "Place of the Greenstone," in 1990 it was extended to include Westland, Mount Aspiring, and Mount Cook National Parks. Incredibly, the whole area stretches over 2.6 million hectares, or in simpler terms, ten per cent of New Zealand's landmass. But what I'd really come for, if nothing else, was to experience some of this massive wilderness and get out onto the remote, protected post-glacier valleys flooded by the seas; Milford Sound and the lesser known and more difficult to access Doubtful Sound.

My phone alarm rings at 4:30AM the next morning, and by 5am I've pulled on my shorts while a mini-van has pulled up outside. I climb in with a handful of other sleepy people. The plan is to be driven the 120 kilometres along Highway 94 to Milford Sound, reputed to be one of the world's most scenic highways, then at sunrise, with sea kayaks, paddle the sound's full length to the Tasman Sea. This would also all depend on the weather, but we were anticipating to be on the water for about five hours, with a support boat bringing us and the kayaks back, as we'd then be going against the tidal currents.

It's still dark when we leave Te Anau, but as the first light starts to appear, the road starts to penetrate deeper into the mountains and into sub-alpine wonderland with streams flowing through the fields and waterfalls dropping down from the mountain sides. As fuel is not available between Te Anau and Milford and with a 240-kilometre roundtrip you need to ensure you have sufficient fuel. That's another reason I'd decided to leave the driving today to someone else and have a chance to view the scenery. Civilization just seems to be disappearing.

It's then we reach a narrow, pitch dark, rough, and pebbly very long tunnel. It's not lit inside as we enter, and seeing how close we are to its walls, it only seems to have enough width for one lane. This is confirmed by our driver constantly leaning forward and looking for oncoming vehicles, which hopefully at this time of the day are zero. Apparently, later in the day and during peak periods, traffic lights will dictate one-way traffic. So this is the impressive 1.3 kilometre long Homer Tunnel, completed in 1953, which passes directly through the mountains to Milford Sound. But it was in 1889 that mountaineer and explorer W. H. Homer originally discovered the Homer Saddle and thought it very feasible to create a tunnel to form a route from Lake Wakatipi (Queenstown) to Milford Sound. Construction took almost twenty years but would ultimately make it the best known fiord here and the only one which can be reached directly by road. Ongoing maintenance is needed to stabilize the rock and divert water, which still flows in through the roof!

The men who built the Milford Road and The Homer Tunnel in the 1930s were, for the most part, victims of the depression, 'directed' to the job by the government.

For the men of the road and those women who followed their men into this wilderness, life was harsh beyond belief, but road and tunnel must go through so they lived it. Small town civilisation was many hard hours' travel away, rates of pay were pitifully meagre and there were no amenities.

The terrain ferocious, high in altitude, steep and rugged, beset by floods, Antarctic snow and ice and deadly avalanches. The Homer camp was so hemmed in by the high Alps that it saw no sun from May to September.

In July 1936 the air blast from an avalanche wrecked a partially completed building near the portal, killing a tunneller and injuring several others.

The following year another avalanche blast wrecked more buildings, killing an engineer and tunnel overseer who, it is rumoured, were discussing the workmen's refusal to work on the grounds that the avalanches were too dangerous.

From The Men of the Milford Road *by Harold J. Anderson.*

Today a sophisticated avalanche programme enables the road to remain open with optimum safety to road workers and users alike. Most avalanche activity occurs during or immediately after a storm and usually affects the Milford Road between June and November.

But oh my, on this pitch dark morning the roads are so intimidatingly cloud covered, wet, steep, and winding that I feel there's no way I could have come on the bike.

We finally arrive at a small water inlet, where we're briefed, changed into all-in-one yellow waterproof jumpsuits, and finally with our paddles, push ourselves out onto the water. I'm teamed up with Jake, a young New Zealander, who I'm glad to see has good arm muscles. Daylight is now starting to appear, with the rising sun revealing the majesty of this place. With the four other two-man kayaks and our leader, Ben, in one of them, we set off and out to the vast expanse of tranquil waters, initially looking out and upwards to the iconic, triangular pinnacle of Mitre Peak, which soars up and disappears into the clouds to 1,690 metres in height.

As we paddle further out, it's here for the next handful of hours that our jaws are left permanently open in undiluted awe. As we silently paddle out, this is truly idyllic, and with no other water vessel out, we have this magical place all to ourselves. But it's also misty, with drizzling clouds suspended over the giant cliff sides that tower over us.

Ben quickly paddles up. "Amazing isn't it? The Maori would often refer to the mountain terrain in the Fiordland region as Ata Whenua or 'Shadowland'—a land so high and sheer as to rarely permit the sun through every valley, and when it did, to the continual different shades of light. We're soon going to see this massive waterfall crashing down the cliffside where we're gonna kayak behind it—amazing!"

Unsurprisingly, by the end of the day, he'll have worn out the word amazing, using it a trillion times. The kayaks continue to silently cut through the motionless water, and every one of us are mesmerized by the pure unadulterated beauty around us. There's just nothing to say but to continue gasping in awe around this mystical cloud covered place.

And it's true that cloud now fills the valleys of Fiordland, just as the glaciers once did. Up until 14,000 years ago the land was smothered by one giant mass of ice. With the end of the last Ice Age, the glaciers retreated, carving out these steep-sided valleys all the way to the sea floor. And with up to ten metres of rainfall annually and over 200 rain days per year, this extreme volume of water has shaped the topography and ecology, providing the unique Fiordland rainforests.

It still houses New Zealand's only original mammal, the bat! Once found throughout forested areas of New Zealand, the short-tailed and long-tailed bats became severely restricted in range during the twentieth century as the country's forests were increasingly felled and bat colonies were attacked by introduced predators such as rats, stoats, and cats. The short-tailed species is threatened with extinction and survives only in small isolated patches of native forest here. It reminds me of that night in Somerset last summer when Lulu and I saw bats freely flying over us and across the fields.

From the silence, Ben shouts over the water, "It's amazing; look! Can you see those young, male seals sunning on the cliffs? They also need to get fat to be able to confront bigger males for females in the future. But for now, it's more like a boys' bachelor party. Amazing!"

I'm glad Jake's behind steering the kayak, as after more than fourteen kilometres of vigorous co-ordinated paddling, my arms and lower back are starting to ache just slightly.

"OK guys, come on over; I've got one last treat. It's going to be amazing! See that massive waterfall crashing down? Well we're gonna kayak through the water on one side, go behind it, and out again on the other side. Amazing!"

With the last party trick completed and us totally soaked, we smile and lazily lie back on the boats and let the bobbing current drift us slowly to a waiting boat, where a guy reaches out to grab us and haul the kayaks on deck. I'm so very happy that my experience of Milford Sound was just above the level of the waters, enveloped within it and making us all feel so very tiny and insignificant in this massive place. And I'm glad that there was no noise from a boat's engine with the noisy chattering of tourists on its crowded deck high above these crystal clear waters. This was truly perfect. Totally exhausted, we finally reach land, pull off our waterproof suits, and are driven over to the main area over the hill facing Milford Sound, where all the masses of buses stop to drop off and pick up. And what another world we encounter with hundreds of people waiting for the first boat of the day. Our little group of kayakers just smile, knowing that what we've just done is priceless and unimaginable to most people.

The next journey will hopefully be even more spectacular to discover the even remoter Doubtful Sound that still has no direct road access. So the following morning I hop onto the local bus heading to Lake Manapouri, the gateway to both Doubtful and Dusky Sounds, where a boat is waiting to take a bunch of us across the first stage of the expedition. It's amazing to think that Manapouri is now the largest hydro power station in New Zealand. 176 metres below lake level, the massive turbines operate, and although normally open to visit, today it was unfortunately closed. This was a massive project, when in 1904 a vision was made for power generation that would involve drilling through ten kilometres of Fiordland mountain. At this stage it was beyond imaginable, but later in the 1960s that all changed, with the massive project being completed when the aluminium smelter near Bluff needed a large, permanent supply of energy. But the project was challenging and sixteen men died, either underground or on the Wilmot Pass. Trucks had to reverse out of the tunnel, which could take up to seven hours. But the result was incredible, resulting in this massive underground power station.

After a breezy forty minutes sailing over the lake, with the snowy topped Cathedral Mountain Range behind us, we're led onto buses. Almost immediately, with our safety belts tightly pulled down, we start winding our way through a narrow unsealed road surrounded by luxuriant tropical vegetation, only climbing higher and higher until we reach the famed Wilmot Pass. Construction took two years to climb up and over the 671-metre high pass. Incredibly, in 1965 the unsealed road was completed in time to transport the machinery from Doubtful Sound to the Manpouri Power Station. With the station complete, the road also began to be used for visitors to access this isolated location. It's the only road on the New Zealand mainland not to be connected to the rest of the network.

Travelling further into Fiordland, the whole place is magical, with rain soaked moss gardens on the cliff sides, towering waterfalls, and mesmerizing views that start opening up around us and providing tantalizing glimpses far below to the waters of Doubtful Sound.

When Captain James Cook got close to its entrance in 1770, he decided on the name "Doubtful Harbour". That's because, fearing he wouldn't be able to sail the Endeavour back out, he resisted entering the inlet and instead continued on around the island. Hopefully he didn't regret not pushing further in, but it was only a lot later in 1793 that the Spanish exploration expedition with the hydrographer Felipe Bauza first properly charted these waters. And with this, it was only a few years later in the 1880s that sealing arrived in New Zealand. And Doubtful Sound's Grono Bay, with a station, helped sealers access nearby colonies on the Nee Islets and Shelter Islands. It's hard to describe now, with the world becoming so politically correct, but the New Zealand Fur Seal proved valuable for its blubber, which was made into oil for lamps, and its skin used for clothing. A lot was shipped back to the London markets. But the frenzied nature of the early trade was not sustainable, and by 1946 the hunting of seals was finally banned.

As we walk to the water's edge, we're once again greeted by the natural silence in this vast fiord three times longer than Milford Sound. There's a strange feeling that we're going back in time, witnessing a unique place that is still practically untouched by man. For the rest of the day we sail along its rugged peaks, verdant rainforests, and twisting, hidden inlets. At one point we just stop, turn the engine off, and experience that unimaginable perfect sound of silence. Anyone who has travelled here will recognise why the Maori name for Doubtful Sound, Patea, is so appropriate. Translated it means "The place of silence." That sense of solitude and serenity sweeps over everybody, and as if in an open church, I pray for everyone I know for their well-being and safety.

And for Maori it's even more of a sacred place. According to Maori legend, the fiords of this area were created by the god Tu-Te-Raki-Whanoa for providing refuge from the stormy seas nearby. He came from the south and worked his way up the island. With a magical adze, he split, cut, and axed the rocks open to let the sea rush in. In Doubtful Sound four young sea gods assisted him, using their own adzes to carve out the four arms—First Arm, Crooked Arm, Hall Arm, and Deep Cove.

That sense of solitude, beauty, and wilderness is further enhanced the next day when I set off from the "Walking Capital of the World," Te Anau, to trek part of the famous sixty-kilometre Kepler Track. Although I only manage a thirteen-kilometre amateurish tramp—through the beech forest along the shoreline and into the pre-historic moss covered forests with their bracken covered floors further up into the hills—there's a feeling that these are still like lost and forgotten jewels of our planet.

I've without doubt been energized for the next leg of the two wheel journey tomorrow to finally find my own mysterious paradise.

16

HELL VERSUS PARADISE

FIGHTING WINDS—DEVIL'S STAIRCASE
CHINESE RESCUE—PARADISE FOUND

Te Anau disappears from the rear view mirror as the bike and I travel eastwards across the Whitestone River pass and into the beautiful, giant flat plains bordering the Eyre Mountains. But no more than thirty minutes down the road and I'm back to feeling miserable and frightened for the two habitual reasons that have haunted me throughout the past couple of months.

Firstly, I have no idea that today is yet another public holiday, this time the Chinese New Year, and what impact it will have, but all I can see overtaking and driving crazily towards me are multitudes of impatient MAUI and STARRV rental campervans and crammed tourist buses. Through experience now, I know to be careful and keep away from the centre line. A large warning road sign also jumps out and shouts, "Keep to the left. It's that simple!" and another one screams out, "Expect the unexpected." Although we're all travelling through a beautiful remote area,

Highway 94 also just happens to be the connecting link from Fiordland to Queenstown, where I'm heading. Queenstown is New Zealand's premier commercialized resort town known for its adrenaline fuelled activities and crazy night life, and which I was keen to just pass through.

Secondly, and probably worse still, I was being physically buffeted by some of the strongest winds I'd ever experienced. I remember once someone saying that as a biker if you had the choice between rain or wind, rain would definitely be your better friend. Out on these massive, wide open plains with the mountains on either side there's simply no protection. Just to keep my balance from the ferocious strength of the wind coming towards me and then battering me I have no other option but to reduce my speed dramatically to a manageable forty kilometres an hour. Yes, I know it sounds ridiculous, but it feels physically impossible to go any faster. The chilly, angry gusts are unrelenting, and I'm seriously thinking I'll be knocked off sideways. The concentration to keep upright on this heavy machine is far from enjoyable, but on the other hand, I'm paid back with at least straight roads and million dollar scenery!

I hate swearing, but shit, this is no good. I can't bear this effing traffic. When is it ever going to effing stop and leave me alone? Again, due to the isolation and distances between places, there's nowhere to stop and catch my breath. I start thinking of positives to keep me going: my home in England, the beautiful places in Wales, and my main objective for the whole journey in somehow finally getting to Paradise in New Zealand. I'm now so close to it, but could this place still be impossible to get to and just something in my imagination? Those three things keep me going.

It's not until I reach Mossburn, the little town of 200 people with the West Dome and Mount Hamilton as its back drop, that I pull over next to a general store serving the habitual and welcoming hot drinks. Now that's a good idea, plus no doubt, they'll have a loo! I place my helmet over the mirror and walk in with the door rattling its little bell to attract attention. A young Chinese guy appears from underneath the counter and, seeing I'm wearing biking gear, gives me an extra wide smile.

"I'd love a coffee, please, and maybe one of your scones. There's a lot of traffic out on the roads today. They all seem to be rushing somewhere."

He slides the mug of coffee over to me. "For sure. It's gonna be mega busy today because it's the holidays; it's a Friday, which doesn't help, and also because it's the Chinese New Year today, so everyone is getting away for the weekend!"

I sigh deeply. I've done it again and chosen another public holiday to travel distances.

"I'm riding over to Queenstown, where everybody seems to be coming from, and then over to Glenorchy. I'm just hoping things will quieten down."

He nods wisely then utters what I don't want to hear, "I ride motocross bikes, but hey, I'd be shit scared riding even those bikes on the roads around here with the buses coming towards you. Be careful. There have been a lot of major accidents here, what with the tourists and people speeding. I was even caught up in a pretty bad one last year with the other woman's car a write off!"

I gulp my coffee down and take on board what I've just heard, and with that, he waves me off. Just as I'm pulling my helmet back on, I notice a guy driving his rental car with one hand while nonchalantly eating an ice-cream with the other. I nod to myself, agreeing to be on the lookout and to be extra vigilant. At the major junction with Lumsden, before heading north on Highway 6, I pull over for petrol and to also pull on another layer. Next to me is a big touring bike with a small Asian guy filling the tank and an even more petite Asian woman rubbing her hands warm.

I give the normal smile, and the guy reciprocates when I ask, "So where are you heading? I'm riding over towards Queenstown."

The guy nods and with a strong Chinese accent jabbers frantically, "We here on holiday, from Taiwan. We from Queenstown and motorbiking all the way to Milford Sound today. You likee here?"

I gulp as I hear that. Oh my god, they've got a massive long trip that I personally would not want to do. That tortuous mountain road down to Milford Sound is probably one of the most frightening for the number of switchbacks and sharp hairpin turns. And that's if you can see them through the low-lying misty clouds covering the mountains. Add to that the amount of cars, campers, and buses on this public holiday on that narrow road and that long pitch dark tunnel; they'll need to be careful. But everyone to their own, and I have total respect.

The last thing I want to do is frighten them, but I do want to warn them. "Make sure to be safe. Ride very careful. People go fast on the flats and round the bends here."

His eyes widen with a surprised look, and he simply replies nodding, "Oh, that's good to know. Thank you. We will!"

I nod goodbye, start up, and turn onto the pleasant, straight Highway 6 with ever more mountain peaks soaring up around me. Some of the fields have already been harvested, with hay bales dotted around, and tempting signs like the "Hunny Shop" unsuccessfully try to veer me off course. Before too long, I catch the first glimpses of the enormous sea-size Lake Wakatipu, with its massive mountains dropping straight down into the deep, deep waters. Giant rain-laden clouds are also starting to sweep across the waters. The lake will remain closely to my left side all the way up to Glenorchy.

I continue on until I stop at a wide layby to take a better look. I've stopped at aptly named Devil's Staircase. I carefully look over and notice it dramatically drops vertically down into the wild lake. The shadows of the brooding storm clouds move across the mountains creating a kind of animation to reveal then hide the deep, dark hidden valleys and humongous rocky cliffs reaching up to the sky. But it's the wind that is once again starting to increase, and the little "white horses" on the lake's surface are starting to appear, spreading out across this watery landscape.

Orange road signs at every bend warn of tumbling rock debris, another gentle reminder for me to literally keep my eyes on the road to avoid any rubble that may have fallen. Close to the airport, I turn to finally follow signs to Queenstown, and in a blink of an eye, I'm riding through heavily congested streets, which could pretty much be anywhere. Smiling, happy-go-lucky tourists are lining up at ice-cream parlours and fast food joints, while hundreds of others are zig-zagging their way through each other to simply just navigate up and down the pavements. I smile and, without even stopping, let them get on with it. From where I've come from this just feels too built-up and "organized" for me.

I have only another forty-five kilometres to get to Glenorchy. The Glenorchy Road I'm now on officially opened in 1962. Road construction began at Glenorchy, and eventually the locals pushed it right through to Queenstown. But up until then the only access to the little settlement was by boat. The steamers serviced all the stations around the lake, and the railway track from its wharf to the wharf shed was the shortest length of railway in the country. The steamer would come in on Mondays, Wednesdays, and Fridays, which still reflects the current mail schedule.

So from what I'd experienced so far, and seeing it was just about half an inch of straightish road on the map, getting to Glenorchy should be fairly hassle free. But soon I'd see this couldn't be further from the truth. Luckily for me now, the traffic had dramatically lessened, and almost like magic, most of the impatient drivers would just automatically overtake—even if they were a bit erratic with a sudden foot down on the accelerator—and disappear.

But very quickly the wind violently arrives from across the lake in frightening, superhuman strength, creating giant, roaring seahorses crashing way below into the rocks. And even worse, the wind's coming directly in from the north, which means it's buffeting straight into me and into the front of the bike. These sudden winds and gusts feel like they've got more of a cyclonic force and kick than anything I've experienced so far. I have no shelter. I am literally on the edge of a high cliff side trying with all my strength just to keep the heavy bike from blowing over.

The unimaginable strength and force of the wind has almost brought my bike to a total standstill. Almost at the top of an unprotected cliff top, I'm literally no longer able to move the bike forward. It comes to a stop. I now have to put my feet down. I'm shaking with fear. It's like nothing I've ever experienced before. The wind is battering me and almost knocking me over. I'm scared shitless by being in such a vulnerable place, where at any moment another vehicle could come up and crash into me. I have no other option but to stay motionless in the road and just fight to keep the bike standing up.

But no more than twenty metres further up I, incredibly, see a layby. But that's not what gives me hope, as just trying to get there and then put the bike on the stand would be a feat in itself. And it would no doubt get knocked over onto its side, or worse still with me underneath it. No, it's the sight of two very ordinary looking mini-vans that are innocently parked horizontally next to each other while their passengers are cocooned inside, unaware of the dramas unfolding outside. I immediately think of shelter. If I could somehow paddle the bike with superhuman strength up towards the top of the ridge and park up alongside them, I'd be sheltered from the raging winds and have a moment to think of what to do next. But I can't move. I'm stuck. With no other option, I desperately start to shout and scream out against the battering wind for someone to impossibly hear me from inside their protective shells.

"Help! Help! Please help me!"

But the screaming must be getting lost within the thunderous noise of the wind. Even taking just one hand off the handlebar to wave and attract their attention is almost too much of a mega effort and risks the bike falling over—and anyway, did I see them only casually wave back? Only a few other cars overtake, look back at my desperation, but simply drive on. Even a few of the people from the two parked up vans, and who all look Chinese, have carefully walked over to the cliff side but don't look behind and walk those few metres to see me. I'm at stalemate. Maybe I should just leave the bike to fall over. My inner palpitations have increased, and I can now almost feel my heart jumping through my jacket. It's only now I find some lost inner strength and step by step over what feels like a lifetime, heave the bike up alongside the first campervan to only moderately shield it from the murderous winds.

But this unimaginable horror scene becomes further amplified as I hear their engines start up, knowing they're just about to leave me on this high unprotected precipice.

For one last time, almost looking into the driver's window, I shout, "Help! Please help me!"

Losing control, I burst into tears. Not for the dramatic effect but just because I feel so totally helpless. This is hell. A Chinese guy slowly and cautiously opens his door and unbelievably gets out. Somehow I manage to explain, mostly in sign language, that I need a couple of people to help hold the bike steady while I'm on it. And the only solution I see is for them to keep holding onto the bike and walk down the hillside with me on it. In that way, if nothing else, I'll be more sheltered lower down, and then ultimately if I still can't continue, it will be easier to abandon. I believe he can see the desperation in my eyes.

"Please Sir, help me. I just need two of you to help me get down the hill. I'll even pay you!"

Yes, you heard correctly. I'm so desperate that if their time is that precious, and my situation so dire, I'm happy to pay them some reward.

He smiles, now understanding, but vehemently shakes his head to the monetary offer, "No, no, no. That's not good. But yes, yes, yes we will try to help you. Wait, I need to tell my family what I will do. They speak no English."

At this stage, I think it's only appropriate we exchange names.

And with that, Chang turns around and screams to another man curiously peering out of the window from the other van, "欸，兄弟！快来帮我一下！这个疯狂的妇女需要帮助骑上来她的摩托车" (or for those who want to scream it: "Āi, xiōngdì! Kuài lái bāng wǒ yīxià! Zhège fēngkuáng de fùnǚ xūyào bāngzhù qí shànglái tā de mótuō chē!"*).

The other guy approaches, and almost like a Laurel and Hardy scene, these two naïve guys, who know nothing about bikes, theatrically grab the bike, pushing it almost over, then desperately try to pull it back to re-balance it while I'm trying with all my strength to just keep on it. When the wind dies down for a millisecond, all three of us somehow get the bike down the measly thirty metres or so to the flat part of shoreline road. At that point I almost feel like hugging Chang and his brother, but time is of the essence, and in this sheltered low lying road, I've decided to immediately head off. Amusingly, as I start to leave, Chang won't let go and pushes the bike like that's going to help, while his brother simply waves me goodbye.

---

*"Hey brother, come help me! This crazy lady needs help with her motorcycle"

What a day! After each of these episodes, I keep thinking it can't get any more extreme, and I'm proven wrong. After another tortuous set of "almost falling off" miles with the stormy winds, I enter Glenorchy at the very tip of Lake Wakatipu. The clouds have gathered, and the cold long-awaited rain now starts pelting down. This all feels like freak weather, but at least I'm safe, and all I need do now is find a way to Paradise!

I shelter the bike alongside Glenorchy Motels in Oban Street and, pulling the jacket over my head, knock on the locked front door. I hope someone's here.

A smiling woman carrying a massive pile of sheets appears from around the corner running from the rain. "Hi there. I'm Kath the owner. Can I help you?"

I give a relieved look. "For sure. I've booked to stay with you for a couple of days. I also need to ask a major question. The main reason I came here was to somehow get to Paradise. I just hope it's easier than the hell I've had to get here! I need some help in trying to get there. In fact any kind of help would be good!"

She looks over my shoulder to the big heavily-laden bike, "Well, you won't get there on that. Paradise is twenty kilometres from here. Eight are sealed, but the last twelve are unsealed, but it's the River Jordan you have to cross to get there and can only really be done in trucks and larger vehicles. Most of it is also private land, but there is a road that goes through the valley then continues on to Chinaman's Bluff and the start of the Dart Track, where all the film crews head out to."

I nod, trying to absorb the information. "So how do you reckon I can do it? The horse place here can't offer me anything."

She smiles, starting to understand my predicament. "Well, you do know it's the Chinese New Year weekend, so it's unusually busy here. We have no car rental places, but you might want to go to the local garage to see if any of the mechanics might drive you up for a jaunt. My husband would normally have time, but we're both rushed off our feet this weekend. All the Chinese are on holiday and seem to be here with everywhere booked. Even after the season it's busy here. Before, this place was quieter, with just the odd occasional film crew. But the Chinese are coming in more and more, and as you know, the problem is they can't drive. You may want to try and hitchhike it but be careful. Even here I've heard of loads of bad car accidents along these stretches. No, your best bet is to talk to the locals."

So I wander down the small street, with the beautiful mountains surrounding this little settlement, past probably the remotest rugby club and pitch in the southern hemisphere and poke my head into a garage where guys are busy repairing cars.

"Is there anyway anyone could drive me up to Paradise to take a look around. I obviously don't mind paying someone and the petrol."

An older man with an oily rag in his hand shakes his head, "This is our busy season. Normally, I could have let one of my boys go, but not now. Sorry."

I nod in thanks and see there are about four other shops along the road, so I decide to ask the same question, but the same answer is thrown back at me. A lot also depends on the weather. Ideally, I don't want to make my way up to Paradise and be welcomed by rain and the mountains hidden in cloud.

I sit in the little convivial Glenorchy Café, the former post office, and mull things over with a warm coffee and a doorstep sandwich while watching the only restaurant next door—a noodle bar—welcoming lines of Chinese people waiting to be seated.

Yes, I could hitchhike, but I'd also need to find a way back, and I had no idea if there'd even be a vehicle up there. I'm so close, yet still so far. All of a sudden the phone buzzes with a message. It's from Kath from the motel. "Try this number. The guy's local and sometimes takes people out. But maybe booked or busy?"

My one hope. I tap in the number. There's only an answering service, so I leave a message basically saying I'll be flexible in the coming days in travelling to Paradise with him, and this was my key highlight to the massive trip I'd just done around New Zealand. It's not until the red rays of the sun have set and I've eaten a hearty meal in front of a cosy burning log fire at the Glenorchy Hotel that my phone finally rings.

"Hey is that you, Zoë? This is Alan. Sorry I didn't get back to you, but I was trying to sort a way to get you there and get special access to the private Paradise 'Arcadia' estate. That's because I know the owner, and I've only just received a reply from him that we can do it. So if you're up for it, I can collect you tomorrow afternoon!"

I'm almost speechless, and with that, raise my wine glass to the bartender for a well- deserved top up.

The following morning, and without much surprise, it's raining hard but at least no goddamn wind. Then almost miraculously, for a couple of hours' respite, at midday the clouds disappear and are replaced by bright, blue sunny skies. It's warm, and the whole place looks completely different as a big white jeep pulls into the motel's driveway. The passenger door is opened from the inside, and a stubbly chinned guy in jeans and T-shirt leans over to shake my hand.

"Hi, I'm Alan. Can you believe how lucky we are? Let's get going before it all changes again!"

To say I'm excited is an understatement, and as we reach the unsealed road, the beech forests have changed to rolling farmlands. Entering Mount Aspiring National Park, we drive over water passes, past Diamond Lake, and enter more and more green farmland. A large, white solitary farmhouse appears embedded in the fertile cow and sheep grazing fields.

Alan points over to it, "So that's Arcadia House. Arcadia is Greek for paradise, like the place. It was originally built in the late 1800s with its 300 hectares of land by Patrick Fenn to attract his fiancée to New Zealand! In the early 1900s it became a hotel, which attracted pioneering tourists who liked the wild life and a bit of shooting. But it's now Jim Vint's place, whose father bought it in the 1940s, and who's granted us exclusive access onto his private land. He owns this entire valley for as far as the eye can see. We'll go drive up through that locked gate and to the top of the hill."

I gasp with delight as Alan steps out of the truck and unlocks the gate to Paradise. I open the window and all I can hear are the remote echoing sounds of contented cows and sheep grazing in this luxuriously fertile place and flying bird songs. The truck stops, and we climb to the top of a green hilly slope that reveals a magical 360-degree view across the massive valley surrounded by snow-capped mountains and a large expanse of flowing river. I simply sit on the soft golden sun-drenched blades of grass and listen to the peaceful silence only interrupted by the intermittent chirping of birds. This is another world, and I don't want this moment to ever end. Its beauty is beyond description, and to be totally honest, I'm feeling a little emotional.

I have reached Paradise.

Alan pulls out a piece of paper from his jacket as we sit silently looking out. "Thought I'd read this to you. It's a note from a Glenorchy local, Christine Kelly, from the local newsletter. Sums it up a bit—

> *You can never "get" to Paradise, it's a state of being, it is the way you feel about things. Some places make it easier for you to feel that way. Paradise is that place 'cos it sends shivers down your spine and it seems far too immaculate to be true. When people ask where Paradise is, I laugh and say—it's just a paddock, you drive and follow the signs, 30*

*minutes to the road's end—And I remember what it is
like; those mountains formed beautifully, like a coiffured
woman looking down at you, the braided river bed, wide,
energetic, windswept, the combination of snow fields and
raw rock, the height of those tops. The intensity of the place
and the transitions it exposes you to. If there is a heaven on
earth Paradise has to be close.*

We finally leave, and as we drive back through the valley, Alan
continues, "No one can say with certainty how Paradise got its
name, though it's true within the area you have the 'Rock of Eden',
'Heaven's Gate', and we've already had to cross the River Jordan to
get here. But some also say Paradise just simply gets its name from
the Paradise ducks we have here! But people came here a long time
ago. There's an old Maori camp near the Dart Bridge, which was
once inhabited by the Maori people who came from coastal villages
in search of Moa, but the main attraction soon became Greenstone
(Pounamu), where it was found in the Routeburn, Greenstone, and
Dart Valleys. In the early days, Greenstone was used for tools and
weapons and soon became a big part of Maori culture. You could
also say this is the real *Lord of the Rings* place, where its film crews
came to film parts of it. I've heard other crews are currently out in
the area beyond Dart River."

As we drive through the valley, Alan continues, "But even this
place has changed. And it's not even in the last ten years. No, it's
just over the last five years that things have dramatically changed

with the Chinese coming. They have all the money. And with the road access now this place will never be the same."

But all the same, I wind the window down and breathe in one last gulp of this perfectly clean and peaceful air from Paradise, and we happily leave. This journey through New Zealand, with its unexpected twists and turns, has all been worth it, if only for these precious couple of hours. But it's also brought home the fact that actual Paradise really is a state of mind. It's not really any special place, but more where your heart is and those emotional bonds with loved ones. It's where you feel safe and secure. My little home on the other side of the world is just as much a paradise as here.

And during the next few days there's nothing much I can do, as it doesn't stop raining, with the scenery forever covered in cloud. On the last day, I stroll past the Glenorchy war memorial statue and stop in disbelief. Things have come full circle from where I started in Walton, my home town. I read one of the inscriptions.

Driver William McIntosh died at Walton-on-Thames Hospital, London on 21 February 1916 aged 30 and was buried in Walton. William served in Gallipoli and was wounded in 1915. He worked as a miner and discovered scheelite on Mt. McIntosh, named after him.

Although not widely known, Glenorchy depended on the scheelite industry as an important economic source for quite some time, particularly in periods of global warfare, as it carried the mineral tungsten, used to harden steel. Scheelite was mined in a variety of places surrounding Glenorchy, including Paradise, which was one of the busiest mines during World War Two. So this brings home even more the reason why my home town of Walton-on-Thames is so strongly inter-twined with New Zealand.

That night, as I start packing to leave the next morning, I overhear some very unwelcoming news on the television—"West Coast braces for Cyclone!"

That's where I'm headed for tomorrow!

"A state of emergency could be declared as early as tonight if predictions about the intensity of Cyclone Gita hold true. The storm, which caused havoc in Tonga last week, has the South Island in its firing line! Its centre is predicted to make landfall late tomorrow. This is bigger and more powerful than ex-tropical cyclone Fehi, which caused extensive damage in early February!"

I gulp at these facts, and once again worry overtakes my thoughts about the incalculable strength of the incoming cyclone, the wind that will start coming in tomorrow, and having to bike back along that treacherous stretch of mountainous shoreline road. Should I stay put or leave mega early to try and get past the lake, and if all else fails, stay in Queenstown, or soldier on and try to get to this remote place I'd chosen up in the Crown Range towards the West Coast before the storm hits? Mysteriously, for most of the day it had been spookily calm before, we all knew, the storm would be hitting.

Later that evening, Kath and I are drinking wine together up in her flat. "Well Zoë, I just don't know what's happening. I've never heard of having cyclones in the South Island. But whatever's coming is gonna be big. It seems like Cyclone Gita has already lashed the Pacific Islands, and it's bringing a significant storm to the country over the next few days as it reaches land. I'm also leaving early to Queenstown, so you could always follow me. But I'd say, being the ever optimistic, that the wind will probably go elsewhere, or if nothing else, will push you from the back, so this time you won't be fighting against it."

Those palpitations have come back to haunt me later in the evening, and I just keep repeating the wish that the wind will be on my back!

17

EMERGENCY SHELTER

CROWN RANGE—CYCLONE GITA LANDS
MAJOR DAMAGE—ABANDON PLAN

I endure an almost sleepless night, tossing and turning, with the nightmare vision of climbing back over the windy mountains to Queenstown, and then if I succeed with that, climbing even higher to more than 1,000 metres through the Crown Range. Although a relatively short distance, this was going to be a challenging ride and, honestly, something I wasn't at all looking forward to.

But at least I did have several contingency options. Kath had said I could stay and wait it out, I could venture to Queenstown and stay there, and finally although only ninety kilometres away, I could tempt fate and ride the whole distance up and through the mountains. Whatever I did, I needed to leave early before the cyclone hit and the country came to a standstill.

Although still dark, the first rays of light are appearing behind the mountains. I am already awake, dressed, packed, and impatient to leave and would only decide when I get to Queenstown how much further I was safely prepared to go.

As I walk out of the bathroom, the news reporter appears on the television: "Cyclone Gita is closing in on New Zealand, and the storm will move over the South Island tonight. A State of Emergency has already been declared in Christchurch, which includes Banks Peninsula. Gale force winds are already gusting up to 120 kph in Marlborough, and heavy rain warnings are in place for Nelson and Buller from 9AM this morning, with 150-200mm expected to fall. Civil defence staff have been deployed to areas expected to be worst affected, and we're advising people of power cuts and road closures. All flights in and out of Wellington will be cancelled from 2:45PM through to midnight due to the severe weather. The TranzAlpine service from Greymouth to Christchurch has been cancelled, affecting more than 1,400 passengers. State Highway 1 is closed north and south of Kaikoura due to slips and rock falls. More than forty schools at the top of the South Island will be closed today.

"People have been advised not to travel during the storm, to prepare emergency evacuation plans and have a grab-bag ready."

At the crack of dawn, I sigh with relief, as there's currently no rain and, more importantly, no visible wind blowing the trees about. I'll leave Glenorchy now. As I approach the bike I'm wondering what it thinks and what it would do. Those are the sort of wacky thoughts you get when you've been travelling out on your own for a while! I start the engine without a problem and, while there's no traffic, head out onto the silent, dark unlit road, with only the first rays of daylight slowly appearing. The lake follows me as I ride up and through the mountains, with the heavy skies framing the views around me. Unbelievably, the only slight breeze is coming from behind and only softly but playfully pushing me along. There is simply no comparison to when I'd ridden the opposite way.

Just before eight, with the sky still dark and the rain now starting to fall, I slowly pass through sleepy Queenstown, still not a hundred per cent decided on what is safest to do. It's only drizzling and nothing massive. The bike is still purring and wanting to move on, which means I won't stop. I carry on down the bizarrely quiet countryside highway and past the turning point to the historic gold-prospecting Arrowtown that on any other day I would have wanted to stop at.

It's then I come to a halt on the side of the road, having to make a big decision. Do I now turn and take the shorter route up and over the Crown Range on SH89 to Cardrona or opt for the safer but much longer detour down to Wanaka and back up the valley to Cardrona? I naively but optimistically look at the only slightly upward incline of the first part of Crown Range Road 89, like that's going to tell me everything. But without further hesitation, I put my foot down. The quicker I can get to this remote place, the better. But for this heavy luggage-laden bike, the narrow road very quickly turns to awkward and steep switchbacks, climbing higher and higher over this cold, cloud laden, tussock high country. Concentration is key on these wet, extreme roads with only short distance views out through to the vast expanses of mountain slopes. I'm feeling I could so easily fall off. With freezing hands, it's not until I reach the highest 1,076 metre pass that the curving mountain road provides some respite and starts to slowly descend towards tiny Cardrona. The quiet settlement dotted along the roadside is comprised of no more than a couple of cottages, a general store, café, and the place I'll be staying at—the iconic Cardrona Hotel.

Not for the first time, I swallow hard and gulp with relief on a safe arrival. I get off outside the historic building and walk into a different world of cosy log-burning fires and welcoming trays of hot coffee and cakes being served to the handful of other travellers reclined back in comfortable armchairs. With open concern on their faces, it looks like they're all deciding on what to do next on this unpredictable morning; to set out or stay put before the storm savagely hits the area. I'm also starting to realize that I'll probably now need to make important contingency plans to escape the current storm's path.

Tomorrow I'd planned to bike a whopping 250 kilometres on challenging mountainous roads, all the way up to Franz Joseph, and start the nine-day leg of the trip along the northerly West Coast. Friends had raved about the area, saying it was nearly all national parks and that it was so pretty it'd make my eyes water! So I'd organised everything, right down to finding the quirkiest, best, and most remote places to stay. I was intending to travel to Ross, where I had friends, and enjoy the Friday Jam Night with the locals at the Empire, stay at Totara Bridge containers on the beach, head to Hokitika Gorge, where another friend and excellent chef had a cool place—Grassy Flat Hut. Then north to Westpoint, which lay on the doorstep of Kahurangi National Park and the coal mining ghost town of Denniston, a few days in lost Karamea, back to Punakaiki for the beaches, then through Arthur's Pass to head back south. Not a lot really!

But at the present moment, and before making all those changes, I was at this beautiful place and wanted to enjoy it. Established in 1863, this place is one of New Zealand's oldest inns and one of only two remaining buildings from the Cardrona Valley gold rush era. Back in the 1860s hundreds of prospectors flocked to the area chasing the miners' dream, and although over the years the momentum of the gold boom dwindled, some men stayed on and persisted as farmers, raising cattle in the valley. In 1926 James Patterson, locally known as Jimmy, became a local legend. He was famous for his attitude in serving alcohol and controlling the amount patrons could drink, depending on which direction they were travelling. Men travelling over the treacherous Crown Range Road were only allowed one drink, while those travelling to Wanaka were allowed two. Jimmy preferred not to sell any alcohol to women. And every winter Jimmy travelled to Christchurch and simply shut the hotel doors, leaving a note—"Beer under counter—help yourself!"

The news on the TV behind the bar is going crazy: "Cyclone Gita is barrelling into New Zealand, with worsening weather due to hit tonight. The West Coast has a heavy rain watch. Severe gale easterly winds with damaging gusts of 130-140 kph in exposed places, which means many campsites in the region have reported full accommodation due to freedom campers seeking a populated safe haven. We are trying to persuade people not to be in tents and to stay away from trees and hollows in the ground. A lot are worried about the storm, with most trying to find alternative accommodation in safe cabins or at backpackers' hostels."

As I see it, and praying the bike doesn't get knocked over outside, I need to stay put for an extra night until things quieten down. So with that, I hurriedly walk up to the reception desk.

"We're terribly sorry, but we're fully booked. There's just no room here. You'll have to somehow get to Wanaka, the nearest place, tomorrow and find accommodation there."

This is not what I wanted to hear, so out of exasperation and maybe a little bit of naïve desperation, I dart over the road to the local café to see if they know of any locals renting a room.

"Well, actually there is a girl who rents behind over there in that little house, but I think they've gone away."

That doesn't deter me as I knock on the door and wait until a long haired student finally opens it.

"I'm looking for an emergency place to stay or just crash down tomorrow night to wait until the storm passes. Any possibility? I could get stranded here."

"Heck. This isn't even my place, and I've gotta lock it up before I head down to Wanaka later. Sorry."

By now it's raining heavily, and as I walk back into the lounge area, the news confirms that roads are being closed up, and towards Franz Josef Glacier, where I'm supposed to be going tomorrow. There're also warnings that for days after, there'll be major problems with any roads that do re-open, with a strong likelihood of possible rock and mud slides, which will cut more roads and communities off. Do I want to risk my well-being and sanity for this last part of the journey? It's no use, I've got to make a quick decision. I agree with myself that I'll abandon this last planned leg of the trip.

If things couldn't get any worse, the forecast now for Cardrona is that snow will arrive here and up in the mountains by tomorrow morning. With now nowhere to stay from tomorrow onwards, I've no option but to, once again, leave early to get to the nearest settlement to avoid this inclement weather. The afternoon is spent calling and pleading for a bed or floor at any hostel, inn, or hotel in Wanaka. Base Wanaka Hostel finally gives me a thumbs up that I have a bed, but only for tomorrow. I'll plan the rest when I get there.

Into the afternoon, with nowhere to go and with everyone around the fire, news spreads that the Kiwis are so desperate that thousands have signed up for a "tongue-in-cheek" event to blow Cyclone Gita offshore to protect the country. The Facebook event "Blow West at Cyclone Giant to Disperse it!" takes place tonight—"Everyone please, Cyclone Gita will be hitting New Zealand tonight and potentially destroy thousands to even millions of homes. We can stop this. We need your help. If everyone can blow north-west at the same time at 6PM Tuesday 20 February, we can counteract the cyclone and reverse all the kinetic energy and save New Zealand."

At 2:55PM the Christchurch mayor declares a State of Emergency for his city! For now I'm just going to forget everything else, luxuriate in their warm spa tub, and indulge in a good hearty meal. But in truth, as I see it I've no other option but to stay close by for the next few days until things calm down.

With the howling wind and rain mercilessly pelting down and battering the windows outside, I'm awake again all night thinking if I'd made the right decision to abandon the north part of the trip and head south. Without a doubt now I'm leaving for the South. I'd be stupid to even try and get to the West Coast, where entire roads were now shut off. And overnight these had increased, including roads heading inland towards me, and which meant the ones I wanted to take. Only early yesterday I could have got to Franz Josef, but now it's shut off. I pull the blanket over my head and try to sleep.

Walking out into the freezing cold, rain sodden morning I heave my bag onto the seat. Incredibly, the forecast was again accurate and across the road snow had fallen seriously onto the mountain tops and splattered down their sides. Thankfully, no white stuff had reached this 1,000 metre high place, also famed for its skiing in the winter, but I could see that the 1,936 metre Mount Cardrona out in the distance was already heavily blanketed. It's hard to believe that just three weeks ago, on 29 January and down the road in Queenstown, it had sweltered under the hottest day in history, reading a sizzling thirty-five degrees! So with no settled snow here yet, I have a window to safely leave.

The bike starts up perfectly. The smooth, flat thirty-kilometre stretch of road through pastureland, and even through the rain, is a surprising joy from what I'd ridden the day before on the other side of Cardrona. I'm shortly riding into Wanaka, park the bike out on the street, and walk into the heaving hostel, with lines of people queuing up to check in and get their keys to their dorms. This feels like an emergency situation, with literally piles of rain-sodden rucksacks and luggage piled in every possible space in the large buzzing reception room. This is not a time to be choosy but just to be grateful of having a bed.

I finally reach the desk. "Hi. I'm booked in at short notice for tonight. But with this storm would you also have anything for tomorrow?"

Behind the counter a girl with frizzy long blue hair screams, "Hell no! It's crazy. We have nothing. Totally booked. Take a look around town and see if you can maybe get something at a hotel. But with everyone who's arrived, accommodation is tight. We just don't have enough of it."

I walk into the dorm and dump my bags down and crash onto the last remaining bed of six, thinking how on earth I'm going to resolve this next little problem! I need to do two things now: find somewhere next to sleep and change my travel plans, cancelling everything I'd already meticulously researched and booked. Three other girls are already in the dorm sheltering from the storm; one from Germany, a student from the West Bank, and another blonde-haired Scandinavian looking woman from Israel, which leads to a very interesting and heated debate later in the day!

With the bike safely parked and hidden behind a shop in a side road, I start walking along the street and into another hostel a bit further up.

Knowing what the answer will be, I ask anyway, "I don't suppose you've got any room here for tomorrow?"

A young smiling guy replies, "Hell no. Nothing. But I will call a couple of places for you, including a friend of mine."

And with that, he generously calls four different places, but everywhere is booked. This is crazy. What am I going to do? It feels like everyone is being forced to change plans. After an hour or so I've scoured the whole place and there's nothing. Heading back to the hostel, I pass a nondescript, little white bungalow just a block away from Lake Wanaka in the downtown district. Was that my imagination, or did I just see an old lady walk past the window? That's it! I know what I'm going to do. I walk to the front door and gently knock on it. I'll take a leap of faith.

The old lady cautiously opens it, and I try calmly to explain my story and that I'll be homeless tomorrow night. With that, Margaret gently puts her hand on my arm, "Well, we can't have that can we? Funny you should ask, but I do have a spare room that I'd be happy for you to stay in for a couple of nights. I love a bit of company. Of course I'd have to ask for something to cover my laundry costs, but it's strange, I had a young chap ask exactly the same only last week! So yes, you're more than welcome to stay!"

The heavy rain continues into the next day when I drop my bags off round the corner at the old lady's house, collect the bike, and park it outside. With this weather there's not much else to do besides a leisurely breakfast overlooking the lake surrounded by masses of campervans, and a visit to the local cinema with Olga, the German girl I'd met at the hostel. Over a beer I learn she has family in New Zealand.

"Prost! Cheers! Good to have met you. Yes, that's right, I'm taking a few weeks holiday around the country before returning to

Auckland to see my family and fly back to Germany. But although this place is pretty, it seems like another place made around tourists, and it's difficult to see anything normal. Even the café workers here are seasonal overseas people."

I nod, realizing more and more that this is a small country attracting a lot of tourists. We wave goodbye to each other, and I head over to Margaret's place. She opens the door and kindly offers me a cup of tea. We sit down in the kitchen.

I hug the warm brew. "If that's OK, I'll take you up on staying the two nights, and hopefully if the weather clears, I'll have a chance to visit the place a bit more. But it feels really busy."

Margaret slowly stirs her tea and nods, "Yes, the weather hasn't helped, and it is peak season. But this place is beautiful, and I love living here, but we have a few problems. There's a lack of accommodation in town. Most visitors are in campers so don't realize, but due to the lack of it, I've heard of and even seen people sleeping rough on our shopping mall staircase and outside next to the supermarket. We need to build more accommodation. And then, I hate to say it, but it's the freedom campers who come and park up anywhere around here with no respect. The district council has introduced wheel clamps for those parked illegally overnight at the Wanaka lakefront. There's a $200 fine plus another $200 if a clamp's used. The problem is they're dirty, leaving rubbish and using the place as a toilet. I've heard the council is trying to find funding for more roadside toilet facilities and ways to crack down on the irresponsible minority of these freedom campers, while wanting to support those who play by the rules and respect our landscapes and special places."

I look back in honest shock, not having realized the extent of it all, but remember those two lovely Dutch women I'd met back in Beach Haven on the North Island. They'd just bought an old battered VW van, from another traveller, with no wash facilities and were going to travel around in it for a couple of months.

Margaret wisely continues, "Not many people know this, but twelve years ago New Zealand had just 350,000 tourists a year. Today we have more than ten times that—3.5 million people come to visit each year, and the hotels and roads just can't keep up. The surge in numbers of these campers has also resulted in overcrowding, risks to public health due to human waste, and what

I find terrible is damage to the environment, with people bathing and washing dishes and clothes in lakes and rivers, including here on the Wanaka lakefront. There's a public outcry, and freedom campers need to stay in properly self-contained campervans. Hopefully, something will change."

What a difference a day makes. I wake up to bright blue skies and a hot summer's day. But the storm has hit hard, roads are still closed and so my new plan is to now head back to the one place that originally fascinated me—Oamaru. I'll stay there for a least a handful of days before getting back onto the original schedule to the old French settlement of Akaroa and finally some extended time in Christchurch.

I put my best foot forward and head out towards the beautiful crystal lake, witnessing more clearly now the spectacular and freshly snow-capped mountains wrapped around it. But everyone else seems to have the same idea, needing some fresh air since being cocooned up with cabin fever over the last few days. I approach the famous little Wanaka tree that stands all on its own in the lake. It looks more like a crowded film set, with dozens of people along the lakefront snapping away with cameras on tripods and mobile phones, trying to get as close as possible to this fragile, living thing. It's a tiny tree and reminds me of the one in Llyn Pardarn Llanberis, Wales. All I can hear are those loud Chinese voices screaming and jumping into the water.

But it's also here among the crowds that I meet a smiling, red-lipsticked Asian bride in her long white wedding dress, matching veil, and bouquet of fresh flowers being diligently photographed by a male companion. Amusingly, she's still wearing her big yellow puffer jacket.

I have to go and say something. "Congratulations! You look beautiful."

She flutters her eyelashes and embarrassingly smiles, pointing over to the cameraman. "Thank you. That's my husband taking pictures. We've just got married. We're originally from the Philippines, but we live in Auckland now, and friends said this would be a good place to visit."

I smile, wish them both well, and walk slowly back, but not before passing a sign in both English and Chinese which I read in saddened disbelief: "The Wanaka Tree has taken over 70 years to get to this size! Its branches are fragile and starting to be damaged by people climbing in the tree. To help protect it and leave it for others to enjoy we ask—1) Do not climb in the tree or swing on the branches, 2) Do not attach anything to the tree, 3) Be respectful of others waiting to take a photo, 4) Remove all rubbish—If you see someone climbing in or damaging the tree please report them to the Queenstown Lakes District Council."

I look at the sight, hoping everyone can read. Returning back along the lake, I once again notice something a little unusual. There's a cordoned-off area, and massive willow trees are being sawn down by a couple of guys. What's this all about?

"Hiya. Seems a pity they're being cut down."

A sweating guy looks round and surprisingly answers back with a strong Essex London accent, "We've had to do this, as they've been battered by the cyclone and put people at risk."

"Doesn't sound like you're from around here. How come? I've been travelling around, but some of the places are almost as crazy as London with the drivers!"

He smiles, "Funny. I've just moved over with my girlfriend. I'm a professional tree surgeon. Yea, I agree, my girlfriend works at the local car rental firm, and she tells me that there's at least one major accident and head-on collisions every month. It's bad, but it's purposely not openly advertised, as you can imagine! But everything said, out of the main tourist season this place is fantastic!"

That reminds me. I need to start packing and check the bike over. Tyres are good and nothing's outwardly wrong. Let's just hope the weather's now died down, so I can get out and leave tomorrow to head back towards and across the Mackenzie Basin and down to the Pacific coast.

18

Change Is Good

Lindis Pass—Oamaru Local Banter
Penguins Galore—Wool Buying

So the change of plan with the new route is to head south, take advantage of the guaranteed better weather, and spend some time to get under the skin of a few places I'd initially just raced through. I'd by now ridden through and experienced three post-cyclones since I'd landed in New Zealand; leaving Christchurch on the first day, through The Forgotten Highway in the North Island, and up in the Cardrona Mountains on the South Island. With now just three remaining stop-overs, I felt like I just wanted an easier, more relaxing ride back with time to rest.

But as ever, I was up and out just after dawn, attaching my bags to the bike, wanting to get away from Wanaka as quickly as possible before all the tourist buses started their journeys. I have approximately 230 kilometres to cover but knew today some of it would be fairly extreme. Stopping for petrol on the outskirts of town, I'm glad to see the sky's clear from any stormy clouds, that the wind's now blown itself away, and there's now just a warm, gentle breeze in the air. Just past Wanaka airport, I jump onto Highway 8, which will lead me easterly through Lindis Valley, and it's here I easily glide into top gear, quickly lapping up the distance.

The countryside fields have very quickly changed to a dramatic scene of open sheep-grazed tussock grasslands that shimmer out to the horizon on this sunny but nippy early morning. I contentedly continue heading on this inland route, which will finally lead to the Mackenzie Basin. But I'm also feeling, with the increasing altitude, the cold sharp and biting winds blowing mercilessly across these vast expanses of empty open space and isolation.

All of a sudden, out of nowhere, and directly in front of me, a giant flock of beautiful merino sheep appear, slowly ambling along the road. Hundreds and hundreds of these white fluffy animals are being pushed forward by a jeep, while the driver casually puts his right hand out of the window simply waving me on to carefully ride past and around them all. While some are contentedly nibbling and grazing the roadside grass, most are ambling on and a few look up at me with scary eyes, probably wondering what this other rumbling animal is up to.

The empty road's character is once again changing mood. The valleys are narrowing, with the road starting to wind in and around them. I'm also noticing, with feeling the cold, that I'm climbing ever higher. This is the start of the Lindis Pass, which reaches 971 metres and is incredibly even higher than the 920-metre Arthurs Pass, which I'd intended to come through on the last leg of the journey when leaving the West Coast. Lindis Pass is the highest point on the South Island's state highway network and the second highest point on the entire New Zealand state network, after the Desert Road on Highway 1 in the North Island. Despite all this, it's not even considered one of the alpine passes, as it's located in the dry interior of the South Island.

Although I'd put on multiple layers under my waterproofs this morning, I'm starting to panic just slightly with the increasing extreme cold I'm feeling. Shit, this isn't good. My hands are so cold and painful they feel like they're frozen, and with no feel and being hard to flex, manoeuvring the bike round the curves is becoming increasingly difficult—and in my opinion, dangerous. I feel that I'm losing physical control. I'm in physical pain from the cold but know that stopping would not be a good idea and would lose my momentum. I'm unprotected in this vast open space, so coming to a stand-still would certainly not warm me up, probably making it worse, and there's no one here to lend a helping hand, whatever that may be!

So not for the first time, with raw pain I simply grit my teeth and with stiffened, swollen, numb fingers accelerate away, keeping my head down from the freezing wind. I just hope I'll quickly reach the next closest settlement of Omarama. Some glimmer of hope is finally given when I see a few vehicles pass by and solitary farming buildings start to appear on the outskirts.

After almost two hours from setting out, and now on the junction at Omarama, I finally notice somewhere familiar and welcoming— The Oasis Café Bar & Grill. Feeling like a frozen Yeti, I somehow park the bike up and, with rigid, cold movements, wobble into the only place I know will revive me—the toilets. I hold my hands under the hot water, rubbing them desperately to bring them back to life, forcing them to get some feeling back. Stamping my feet, I'm not quite flexible enough to also heave them up into the sink to soak them in warm water! My red fingers slowly start to move again, as they're then heated up under the drier.

I sit down contentedly for a hearty cooked breakfast and a gallon of coffee and grab a local paper in the warm café. I smile and nod as I read a small piece from Mischa Clouston, a sheep, beef, and deer farmer's wife, about appreciating life here in this remote, far flung part of the country. A message which could so easily translate to other parts of the world—

> *Stop at the top of the farm and look down on what you see; be proud of your creation.*
>
> *Notice the reflection on the sea, river or lake as you drive past.*
>
> *Stop on that bushwalk to notice the sights and sounds around you.*
>
> *Acknowledge someone's lovely garden and tell them if you have a chance.*
>
> *Listen to birds singing in the morning as you hang out the washing before going to work.*

Admire your handiwork on the tractor as you watch the crops begin to grow.

Cheer on someone you know in sport or in a race.

Pulling my jacket back on, I'm also glad to already know that the familiar 120 kilometres of road that I'd already ridden down back in January will be a lot easier, descending quickly into lakeside valleys along the Waitaki Valley, melting into intensely farmed agricultural lands and finally reaching the coast at Oamaru. And this all means that it'll get warmer. I'm feeling a lot better, and after topping up with twelve dollars' worth of fuel ($2.13 a litre) and checking my tyres, I gently and encouragingly stroke the tank, and we're off. As I quickly accelerate and enter the valleys, I again see the storage lakes of the Waitaki hydro scheme, which helps provide a fifth of the nation's power. Each lake, filled by water coming in from a network of canals, is held back by impressive dams, and it's at the 100-metre high Benmore Dam—in the middle of nowhere—that I take a short stop to view this massive eye-popping engineering feat.

Back on the bike, I glance down at my tank bag and take note of the address I need to get to—The Red Kettle Youth Hostel on Reed Street. Entering the outskirts, I fly past Oamaru Racecourse to then only get stuck behind three massive lorries packed with bleating sheep slowly driving down this main thoroughfare onto Thames Street. Thankfully, I've soon turned off, ride up along a quiet road, and park outside a white picket fence and opposite a sweet factory. I've arrived at the Red Kettle Hostel, which will be my home for the next five days. This charming, down to earth hostel looks just fine by me.

A solitary girl with her arms and legs covered in tattoos is sitting cross-legged on one of the four beds with earphones on. She kindly smiles and nods to the rhythm of the music in greeting. I nod and smile back and already feel this is a welcoming, laid-back place, which is exactly what I need. I pull out clean clothes from my bag, having also noted they've got washing facilities here that I'll be using later, and decide to take a wander to stretch those legs.

Already, I can see why this is one of New Zealand's most alluring provincial cities as I walk through its well-preserved Victorian Harbour Street with independent craft shops, galleries, and cafés lined along it. Out on the main street are grand, colonnaded civic buildings, a majestic opera house, courthouse, and museums built of the distinctive cream local limestone, which highlights the town's historic prosperity and makes this place feel very unique. These limestone outcrops throughout the area once provided shelter for the Maori and later raw material for European builders. As a commercial centre for gold prospectors, alongside the quarrying, timber, and farming communities, Oamaru grew in prosperity. Its port also opened for migration in the late 1800s. But like all eras, after the boom, the place withered away, and it's only in recent years that the town's come back to life. I get the feeling that there're probably a lot of stories here that I somehow would like to try and find out about.

I walk through to the harbour, with its bobbing little fishing boats, and promise myself to try and find those elusive penguins that this place is so famous for. Apparently, Oamaru is unique in having both yellow-eyed and blue penguin colonies within walking distance from where I'm standing. But it's only really in the evenings when they come ashore to their nests.

It's then just by chance that I catch sight of a little door tucked away in a small alley with a sign with one of the black and white birds above it. This is The Penguin Club, where they play live music but only on Friday nights! I smile with my luck and make note to come back!

Later that evening Linda, the German tattooed girl, and I walk towards The Penguin's bar and grab two bottles of Mac's beer. The live music has already started playing, and we nudge through the tightly-packed room to the last few remaining seats at a table with a handful of guys, who kindly give a welcoming nod. They're all members of a band: Jeff, a sheep shearer; a taxi driver; and the other an accountant.

I draw a chair closer up to Jeff. "Sounds like you have a hard job. I'm interested to know more."

"Yea. We work our socks off. But go and see my mate, Ross, over at the wholesale wool warehouse on Harbour Street, and he'll, I'm sure, tell you a story or two. Just tell him we met up."

Not for the first time, I take a mental note of the other name and appreciate the kindness of everyone I've met along my journey. It would be interesting to see what really goes on with the wool here and what New Zealand is so famous for.

We all click our bottles together, and Linda leans over, nudging me, "We should also walk along the pier later tonight and see if we can find the penguins. If you're up for it, we can also drive in my car over to Bushy Beach tomorrow to see if we can catch sight of the other ones, the yellow-eyed penguins. But people have told me it's tough, and you need to stay in the hides for sometimes quite a long time. But there're usually loads of seals."

"Sounds good to me. That would be great. So how long did you say you've been in New Zealand?"

She takes another long slurp from her bottle while shifting the chair closer to be heard over the music, "It's a long story, but I'm on a one-year working visa. But it's really tough now to find work. I'm a fully qualified landscape gardener, but what I've learned is that basically New Zealand has no limit on the number of work visas they give to people, which means that finding work is becoming more difficult. It's so tough that I've recently applied for a job just picking grapes. I got an interview, but the guy from the vineyard said he's got more than eighty candidates for just fifteen places. So you know what? He's asking now for CVs and more credentials, like having vineyard experience! You've also got to be highly motivated, work six days a week, ten hours a day, and all we get is the minimum wage of seventeen dollars an hour. All this for just picking grapes! But the good thing is that taxes are not high for backpackers, only 15.5%. I'm waiting to hear back from him tomorrow, so I can hopefully start next week. We'll see!"

At the end of the evening, with our toes still tapping, we walk up along the moon-lit harbour and sit quietly along the shoreline, catching glimpses of a few tiny blue penguins waddling up from the sea and quickly hiding to nest under the waterside buildings.

I'm woken up early the next morning by a loud knock on the door, then an even louder voice shouting, "Zoë, are you awake! This is Gary, who runs the place!"

"I am now. What is it?"

He peeks around the corner of the door. "There's an old guy, who was walking down the street and kindly came to tell me that he saw your bike's rear view light on. He didn't think it looked normal. Maybe you should go and check it."

"Cheers Gary. That doesn't sound good."

I quickly pull my jeans on and, bleary eyed, walk barefooted onto the street to the bike. I can't believe it. When I arrived yesterday, I must have turned the key to the far left, which leaves the rear light on. I put the key in, turn it, and push the start button. Nothing. I push again. Nothing. Even I know the battery is flat and dead. All I can think of it's a good thing I wasn't in the middle of nowhere, needing to leave immediately the same day. Thankfully, after a few calls with the guys back in Christchurch, I'm told they'll get someone local to come over the next day.

So with plenty of time on my hands, I remember what Jeff said last night and wander into town. I arrive at a set of massive, anonymous wooden doors of an old stone warehouse in Harbour Street. One is slightly ajar, so I curiously peer inside and then squeeze through. Thousands of gigantic white square stuffed bags are piled on top of each other to the rooftop.

A sturdy guy with blue overalls walks over, probably wondering why this stranger is here.

"Hi there. I was chatting with Jeff last night, who said to come and have a chat maybe with Ross, who could maybe tell me more about what's happening with the wool here."

He looks at me in amusement, hearing my English accent. "You're in luck. He's just got in from a drive up in the High Country." And with that, he shouts out, "Ross! You've got someone here to see you."

Another sturdy guy, in dirty blue overalls, walks over sticking his hand out, "Hi, I'm Ross Meikle—heard you might be coming over. Only got a bit of time, as we're grading and packing all this wool, but come and take a look."

And with that, he kindly shows me crate upon crate of raw wool of different textures and qualities.

"Here, take a few pieces and feel the difference."

"I'm fascinated. Tell me more. Back home we always associate sheep, lamb, and wool with New Zealand."

He smiles and walks towards one of the giant bales packed with wool. "Where do I start? I'm what they call here a wool buyer but also a sheep shearer and did that for twenty-six years in Australia, New Zealand, the US, Scotland—pretty much anywhere around the world that had sheep! But we all know that the supply is declining from the farms, and I'm having to drive further and further to source the wool. This is mainly due to the government, who gave money to the farms to convert them to dairy, and it's true that most have, with large irrigation systems put in place, and then they sold the sheep off.

"You need to know that in 1982 there were 72 million sheep here in New Zealand. Now it's 27 million. There are too many meat processing places. The price of wool has gone down so much that farmers can't cover the cost of shearing for the wool, so they make their money through the lamb meat. It's sad to say, but wool is just a by-product now."

He walks over and leans against one of the enormous 211-kilo bales. "The value of this bale is just $400. I buy it for $200. In 1990 it was worth, and I'd sell it for, $1000! The decline has been everywhere. In the early 1990s the Scots were actually tipping diesel on the wool and burning it, because it wasn't worth taking to the market. I said at the time to everyone to have faith and that the wool boom would come back again. But I've been saying that ever since, because it just hasn't changed. But I can tell you one thing, if something doesn't happen quick there won't be any sheep!"

And with a saddened face he walks me over to the different wool bales and pulls off three different strands for me to feel. The soft beautiful merino, used for luxury clothing bought mainly by Italians, the thicker half-bred wool for other clothing, and the cross-bred wool, which feels a lot coarser and thicker, used for the carpet trade.

"It's a sad time. We're living in a quick fix, buy, and throw-out consumer society all over the world. No one's darning the wool socks or jumpers like our older generations did for them to last just that bit longer. Now it's the cheap clothes and man-made fibres from places like China where we're told you only have to wear them a few times, as they're so cheap. So like so many places, with core industries declining, New Zealand is turning its main industry more and more to tourism."

"Thanks, Ross. Your honesty means a lot. A lot more than you can imagine."

And with that, we shake hands, and walking away I softly pull down my merino wool beanie I'd bought in Te Anau, wondering for how much longer this wool will stay available.

Later that day, Linda and I drive over to Bushy Beach, and although the views are spectacular down the steep cliff side to a solitary beach, the only movement we see are large seals bathing on the sand and cooling off in the ocean.

Thankfully, the next evening, Tom, who's normally a local fireman by day, appears with a long cable to re-charge my battery from his truck. Those guys back in Christchurch have done good, and with a large grin I wave him goodbye, checking the lights are off and I can start up again!

It's been almost a week since arriving, and walking back across the picturesque Oamaru Public Gardens from my daily swim at the local indoor pool where it's only ever me and local school kids frolicking in the other lanes, I realize this is the last day in a place that has opened its doors to me with open arms. I've even had a few people recognise me with a friendly wave in the streets. Among many others, I've been introduced and welcomed by Mark from the town council and Oamaru

Whitestone Civic Trust, who's recounted stories about its past and what they're doing to restore the place, the people at the town library, who gathered information for me, to Bill who runs the Adventure Book Store, and amazingly the same guys at the whiskey distillery here that I'd met all that time ago at the Burt Munro Challenge in Invercargill. It's a tight-knit community here, but one which is thriving. This is the best unplanned diversion I could have made.

But there's still one main thing I want and need to do before leaving this place and New Zealand. Throughout my journey, I'd seen the beautiful Toki pendants worn not just by the Maori but by so many other free spirits. It's worn as a talisman against evil for the wearer and a guardian of nature and the environment. Each of the thirteen shapes has a meaning, and I knew this would be a good keepsake and meaningful memento of the journey. One of the locals had told me to check out a little hidden place off Thames Street for best prices and sound knowledge on the stones.

The little door-bell rings, and I walk into an Aladdin's Cave of memorabilia and cabinets filled with green stones of every hue. An old bespectacled gentleman is sifting through piles of the same Greenstone.

He looks up and smiles, "What can I do for you?"

"I heard you could help in giving some advice to choose the right toki for me. I've been travelling for a long time, and it hasn't always been the easiest, but what I've gained and experienced from the people and the land here is priceless. I'll never forget this place."

He nods, understanding the importance, "Who would know it, but I'm also a biker for my sins, so understand what you're saying. Toki, but pronounced tuki, means strength and knowledge, which the Maori people strongly advocate. The Maori name for Greenstone is Pounamu and is known here in New Zealand as a symbol of courage and strength in times of adversity. In the beginning toki were just worn by the Maori elders as a symbol of power, wisdom, and authority. The toki (adze) was foremost a chisel tool used by the Maori people of Aotearoa to carve their great canoes and the detail of their meeting houses. They called the stone Pounamu, which refers to the hard, durable, and highly valued nephrite, jade, bowenite, or serpentine stone they found here in southern New Zealand. I'm still able to source some pounamu from locals' land, like Lyn who has a farm just thirty kilometres south of Hokitika. But for people like us, there's more and more of a problem for getting hold directly of the authentic greenstone and an increasing problem of a lot of fake provenance stone now coming in from Asia, which means some people are miss-sold and buy the wrong stuff. And this is all because, and quite rightly so, that all pounamu is now supposed to be owned by the Maori. The Ngai Tahu is the most important tribe of the southern region of New Zealand, and since 1997, when they'd been asking for it back, the government finally returned the ownership rights to them and to act as the guardians of the Pounamu."

He walks over to a pile of Greenstone and rifles through it.

"As I get it direct, it's a lot less than what you'd pay elsewhere. Here, have a look at some of the designs. There's the Eternal Life shape traditionally worn to ward off evil spirits and illness, there's the Koru spiral inspired by the uncurling fern fronds and represents peace and tranquillity, the Single Twist symbolizing the path of life—but what about this piece? See how unusual it is? It's nephrite jade, with the green spots looking like our native river fish swimming through the streams. It's the hardest and one of the most sought after, and it was also dug up from Lyn's farm. I think this Hei Toki of one solid strong piece representing power, wisdom, and authority is maybe stuff you've learned through your journey."

I feel the smooth, beautiful chunk of stone dating back thousands of years, I nod, and with that, he ties its leather cord around my neck. The journey now feels almost complete, and tomorrow I'll be leaving for the last leg of it wearing my toki, which will hopefully help to protect me and provide that inner strength.

As I walk out of the little shop, Graeme calls out, "Forgot to say. You might just catch them as they're about to leave. But get down to the parking lot now on Marine Parade. There's a vintage and classic car and bike meet this morning. My friend, Pete, should be there on his classic Triumph bike."

And true to his word, a startling and surprising array of classic British cars and bikes are getting ready to leave for their little promenade, which also amusingly includes a guy dressed as a policeman wearing an old black and silver custodian helmet on an even older bike. Pete is indeed also sitting on his old Triumph, ready to set off. I introduce myself and, once again, realize how small this place is.

"Hey Zoë! Yes, I heard you were here and what you were doing from my wife, who works with Graeme. She texted you might be popping down. You've been on quite a trip through this country of ours. We're just about to leave for our little club jaunt, but it won't be as far as yours!"

With that, he laughs out loud, pulls his old chin strap tighter, and waves me goodbye. And I'll also be waving this lovely place goodbye tomorrow, not regretting for a moment the storm that made me come to stay here.

19

HOMEWARD BOUND

BANKS PENINSULA—FRANCE IN AN EXTINCT VOLCANO
STOLEN LUGGAGE

I pull my visor down and my neckerchief up and over my chin, kick the tyres, and start the engine, hearing the bike wake up and come back to life. I'm under no illusion, knowing that travelling northwards through this busy section of asphalt will certainly not be the most picturesque or relaxing part of the journey. Since my departure over two months ago I've now clocked up almost 5,000 kilometres. And back on the road, after those handful of rest-up days, it feels good to be moving again. Today's plan is to ride 300 kilometres almost getting to Christchurch but to turn off just before and make my way over to Banks Peninsula to almost reach its tip at Akaroa.

So with the bike contentedly humming under me, I pass through the quiet early morning streets of Oamaru, immediately finding myself back on Highway 1, with the straight road quickly entering flat, anonymous agricultural lands and small townships. It's a warm day with a clear sky and not a sign of any threatening storm clouds or cold rain out on the horizon, which makes me feel totally relaxed. With the bike purring, I kick up the gears and quickly pass the small port city of Timaru and enter the flat plains of Canterbury, where more and more trucks are appearing and fast, impatient vehicles accelerating and racing past me. Incredibly, even in this peak season, there are no other bikes here, and then I realize for that matter I hadn't really seen that many throughout the entire two month's journey!

But soon all that noise and impatience have disappeared. I turn off at Rolleston and enter a pretty little rural road that leads me through a patchwork blanket of green pastures and brown harvested fields to Lincoln and then, six kilometres further, to Tai Tapu, nestled in tranquil woodland at the foot of the Port Hills. It's here I pull off the road to stop at the local gas station then slowly ride down the main street looking for an inviting café.

Leaving the little settlement and now on Route 75, the road continues to sweep through cattle grazing pastures, soon skirting the coast alongside beautiful flat white beaches and then licking the brackish lagoon of Lake Ellesmere. It's then past Lake Forsyth and around hills that are increasingly twisting up ever higher towards the tiny community of Little River. And it's around here that everything dramatically changes.

I've entered Banks Peninsula, an impressive and rugged volcanic thumb sticking out into the Pacific Ocean, which resulted from three violent eruptions from three ancient volcanoes. The Peninsula is cut off from the rest of Canterbury district by two drowned craters with their settlements of Lyttelton and Akaroa. The twisting roads wind unforgivingly along and around the volcano's steep sides, and once again, I've been put into an uncomfortable and defensive mode, worried about my ability to climb these awkward tight bends, already thinking about having to do exactly the same on the way back in the next few days to Christchurch!

But the wild, unspoilt beauty of this unique place, in its equally unique location, is truly astounding as Akaroa comes into sight. Imagine millions of years ago, a New Zealand volcano bubbles up steaming golden goo from the depths of the earth. The volcano finally lies dormant then becomes extinct. Over the numberless years that pass the tides wash in and out and eventually break through the volcano wall, and the sea rushes in to fill the void, creating this waterside town and retreat of Akaroa, or "Long Harbour." It was the Ngai Tahu Maori tribe who first discovered the place a long, long time before even Captain Cook in the *Endeavour* sighted it in the 1770s, believing the peninsula was an island. Fifty odd years later in 1838, Captain Jean Francois Langlois, a whaler and coloniser, traded goods with the Maori for what he believed was the entire peninsula and returned to France to encourage settlers to come and make it a new French colony and whaling port. When they finally returned in 1840 they discovered with shock that the British had already claimed the land. But the French still established a settlement, creating this little French town, with its own French road names and architecture.

Today this place is probably just as well known, if not more so, for the pods of small playful Hector's dolphins and, unexpectedly, what I'd see later—the massive cruise ships.

Slowly descending a small hill, I turn into Rue Julie, then Rue Lavaud, finally parking the bike outside "Chez La Mer." Walking along the pavement and into this backpacker's hostel that was once an old colonial home, I smile, as all I can hear around me are the excited voices of French people chatting away. I hear not a word of English. Crazily I feel, and quite rightly, I've maybe entered a remote French settlement!

I'm led into a small eight-bed bunk dorm but look around in horror, as it looks more like a bombshell has hit it, with clothes strewn and possessions flung everywhere with not a care in the world. There's nowhere to put anything except onto my own top bunkbed. I ominously, but without yet knowing why, notice a mattress has been removed from one of the narrow beds. This place feels just a bit dirty.

The next morning, I'm itching like hell with weeping, scratchy skin spots all over my body. To top it all off, I'd also had diarrhoea all night, necessitating I quickly but awkwardly scramble down from my bunkbed every half hour. Luckily, I'm pretty sure all the other seven snoring room-mates didn't even notice or hear me. I diligently spread the cream I'd been given by Cristina at the vineyard all those weeks ago, optimistically hoping only sandflies are to blame, but I doubt it. More like bed bugs and the reason why I now believe the mattress had been removed. For the first time on the trip, I awkwardly make an official complaint and insist I'm transferred to another room. Luck is on my side, and I carry my stuff into a quiet little room with just two other beds. And although supposedly a mixed dorm, with a friendly train mechanic leaving that day, besides another girl, I have the room all to myself.

The next morning, still scratching my arms and legs, I walk to the Main Wharf, where a hand is held out to help me board a beautiful fifty-foot gaffe-rigged ketch. Built in 1922 in Auckland, this wooden boat is the oldest of its kind in New Zealand. The friendly captain's name is Bill, and for the next few hours with just a handful of other people, we hoist the red sails up and, with just the sound of the wind pushing us forward, head out towards the Akaroa Heads. Sailing out along the vertical volcanic cliff sides and past the little lighthouse, I stare with disbelief across the waters to two gigantic passenger cruise ships with little motor boats starting to ferry multitudes of passengers to the harbour.

The calming feel of the warm morning breeze sweeping across my skin is helping with the itching as I scramble across the deck to sit next to Bill, who's steering the boat. I inquisitively ask, "Those ships are massive, and Akaroa is so small. The town's going to get swamped with all those visitors!"

Bill looks up to the sails, manoeuvres the rudder slightly, and sighs, "Yes, you could say that. This morning we've got two ships here. One that holds 4,000 and the other that accommodates 2,000 passengers. They're here for the day and will leave tonight as part of their trip around New Zealand."

"I wasn't expecting this. I thought Akaroa would be pretty quiet."

He chuckles, "Well at this time of the year not any more. The ships used to dock at Lyttleton, which is conveniently located next to Christchurch, with deep anchorage in that other drowned crater. But sadly the Lyttleton cruise terminal got hit and destroyed from the quakes in 2011, so that means a lot of our daytime peace is regularly shattered with people getting off in town here and then getting back onto lines of buses taking them to Christchurch, or they stay and just mooch around."

"So how long do you think it's gonna last for?"

"God knows. We've recently had news that Lyttelton is spending in the region of fifty-six million dollars for a new cruise berth at the entrance to their inner harbour, scheduled to open for the 2020 cruise season. But that's been put on hold, as they need to refine and assess its impact due to the Hector's dolphins."

And with that we coincidentally start seeing a pod swim up to the boat and start playfully swimming alongside us.

"It's all about the impact of the underwater noise from the build to the marine life, which could cause hearing damage to them. They say they'll scan the area for seals, whales, and dolphins during the pile driving, and if any are spotted, they'll stop work. It's gonna be mega, as the first custom-built cruise ship facility in the country to accommodate the world's largest cruise vessels, and they reckon it would be used by about eighty ships a season. This year alone we've welcomed more than seventy ships, but the biggest one holding 5,500 passengers can't even get in here. It's been past ten times this season, which means ten missed opportunities for people to come and spend money here. But you can see Akaroa's being put under pressure, as our population is only 660. Not surprisingly, Akaroa was voted top cruise port in New Zealand and Australia last season when 147,000 passengers visited."

The dolphins continue to jump and play around the boat.

"Yep. We'll have to see what happens. Now, does anyone want to see a shag!"

We all turn to look at him, not quite sure how to answer that question! We sail towards a rock face where scrawny looking birds, similar but smaller than cormorants are sitting on the ragged ridges.

"There you go! The shag birds!"

Reaching land, the place has changed into noisy, bustling streets, and the pavement-lined cafés are full to bursting.

And I've already made a decision. I'm going to curtail this leg of the trip, leave the day after next, and extend the few days I've got left in Christchurch, which was a place I was initially frustrated I couldn't have stayed longer at.

As I jump down onto the pontoon, I call up to Bill on the deck, "Hey, I forgot to ask. Before I leave, if there was one thing to see here that is a bit off the radar, anything you could suggest?"

Bill rubs his chin, smiles, and points over to the other side of the harbour, towards Children's Bay and up the grassy hillsides. "Go take a look right up there. The "Rhino" Walk should only take you a couple of hours, but you'll be in for a surprise."

I smile. I like surprises and those sorts of curious recommendations, so put my thumbs up and wave goodbye. But tourists aside, this is a pretty place, with the old French cemetery and quaint little residential streets taking you up the hillside, and in the quieter seasons, without the cruise ships, it must be a delight.

The next day, after a croissant or two and a café au lait, I follow the harbour's boardwalk to Children's Bay with its brilliant blue waters and start to head inland up a small forested slope. Weird clicking and tweeting sounds fill my ears, which reminds me once again, that I'm in a distant, tropical land and habitat. I continue making my way up the valley until I stop to see the first view out to the bay below and Akaroa. But what's hiding in the grass ahead . . . .is that a giraffe? Four metal sculptures of giraffes are contentedly grazing in a long grassy field. I continue climbing ever higher, until I reach the top of the hill and see a gate into a cattle paddock. Out on the hill's horizon stands a strange shape. That's not a cow; that's a rhino! I gingerly climb over the fence and walk into the field, seeing how the cows respond. Nothing. They just continue contentedly grazing. Approaching this massive life-size object, I see the rhinoceros has been incredibly made from just old scrap metal, car parts, and components. It stands on this prime position overlooking Akaroa Harbour on one side and Takamatua Bay on the other. There's not a lot that can top this off as I sit back against the rhino listening to the birds calling out with the odd moo here and there and breathe in these beautiful views, with not a single other person in sight!

For one of the last times, early the following morning, I religiously check the bike, heave the bag onto its seat, secure my helmet, fasten my jacket, pull on my gloves, and look down at the weather-beaten road map that's navigated me up and down the entire length of New Zealand. It's going to be a fairly short ride to Christchurch, but varied and scenic, and I'm going to absorb and appreciate every single moment. Although to be totally frank, I'm still shit scared of some of those hairy twists heading back down into the flat valley on the other side of the volcano. And although I reckon it's only about eighty kilometres, I remember so many people telling me along the way that it's not the number of kilometres I need to calculate but the time it takes. And this is all due to the diverse and sometimes difficult terrain, switch backs on the mountain passes, and distances that just didn't seem to be included on the map! So I'm conservatively reckoning a couple of hours.

I turn the key, put my foot on the peg, and twist the throttle. We're off winding back over Banks Peninsula, through the remote harbours, bays, and mountain roads along Highway 75. Although the other alternative route back is up Akaroa Summit Road and around the crater rim, I'd heard the steep road was to be respected, and due to my experience with the campervans, I decided the first and almost equally challenging option would do me just fine. After all, I wasn't here to get medals! The roads are clear, and the only other living things I see awake on this early morning are contented Herefords grazing in the roadside fields.

I stop for one last moment on this empty road, which somehow seems to encapsulate what I've discovered over the past couple of months—natural beauty, the coasts and their pounding seas, and the green hillsides and mountains. A lot of the journey has been totally unexpected, full of surprises that, smiling to myself, I know I wouldn't want any other way.

Christchurch beckons me with a warm welcome, and as I arrive, I ride down those familiar streets with the sun now shining in a cloudless sky. This could be a totally different place from the dark, dismal one I'd arrived at during the stormy cyclone all those weeks ago.

The Jailhouse is my home again for the next few days, which I happily consent to, with my bike safely parked up inside the prison gates, unable to escape. The bike's done me good and performed stoically well through this eclectic country of New Zealand, which has had so many unexpected surprises around almost every corner. I carry my bag—with all my priceless mementos, notes, and possessions in it—leather jacket, and helmet into the store room until I can check in later and get access to my cell.

So for now, all I can do is grab some breakfast at the best local place, the Addington Coffee Co-Op, and take some time to wander around this place absorbing its uniqueness in being a survivor.

Walking along the streets of Christchurch, I look up at the snow-white giant statue of Captain Scott, who died returning from the South Pole in 1912, and I'm emotionally moved when I read part of his diary inscribed into the stone—

I do not regret this journey which shows

that Englishmen can endure hardships

Help one another and meet death with

as great fortitude as ever in the past.

Not far away, I go to sit and reflect on one of the 185 Empty White Chairs, a temporary art installation and remembrance space reflecting the loss of lives following the 22 February 2011 earthquake. Each white-painted chair is different, representing how unique and individual every person was. But from what I've seen, New Zealand has a strong heart and will survive.

Finally, my hunger pangs lead me to the majestic old Post and Telegraphic Office building, where amazingly, pneumatic sliders filled with delicious food are delivered in the original 100 kph pneumatic network around the massive room.

By the end of the afternoon, I'm starting to tire and simply need to rest up and unpack back at the prison. I walk past my bike, fondly patting it, and ask the girl at the reception desk for the key to the store room to retrieve all my worldly possessions. I wander in, look around, stop, look around again, move suitcases around, look into dark corners and recesses, peer up onto top shelves, bend and look under tables, and in fact, I look everywhere. All my stuff has disappeared, including my beloved leather jacket I'd put on top of my bag. This can't be happening. Why am I the chosen one? I know it's a hostel, but surely the nondescript tatty bag wasn't stolen!

I rush back to the counter. "I'm sorry to say this, but all my stuff is missing. Besides my phone, some cash, a credit card, and my sunglasses, I'd left everything there, including my passport. I was told it would be safe."

By now a new girl is working behind the desk and comes with me into the room to look around again. Again, nothing.

She forces herself to find an answer, "Well all I can say is that security is very good here. We only let fellow travellers access this place."

With that, I need to quickly think things over and cross the street to a bar for a drink or two. As the sun's going down, I walk back to the counter feeling totally helpless. A new guy looks up, recognizing something to do with the number of the key I've asked for.

"You're not the girl with the motorbike who's got missing bags are you?"

"Yes, I've got nothing. It all disappeared during the day."

He smiles. "Well, you'll never believe it, but I've got good news for you. Your bags made a trip to the airport. A taxi has just dropped off a bag, helmet, and jacket coming back from the terminal. Take a look behind the counter. Are these all yours?"

I almost feel like hugging him, and although I press him for answers, never do get the full story on how they left before me to the airport. I check inside, and incredibly, everything, including my cherished merino beanie and Toki are still wrapped in my clothes.

Throughout the next couple of days I continue walking down the sunny streets discovering multitudes of wonderful sights: a polo match tournament in North Haggley Park, a dinosaur street mural on Canterbury Museum's Gothic and Victorian façade, beautifully painted containers still stacked up in the empty spaces, the World Peace Bell whose equivalent stands in the courtyard of the United Nations, wooden punts peacefully moving along the Avon River, a rowing boat house that could have a twin in Cambridge or Oxford, a flashing message: "Everything is Going to be Alright" on the Christchurch Art Gallery, and even penguins balancing on top of the Penguin Express bus.

But it's on the very last afternoon of this epic journey, swallowing the fact I've biked over 5,000 kilometres on my own around New Zealand in some of the most extreme conditions, that I have one of those enlightening moments. For some extra peace and inspiration, before dropping my bike off and starting my long journey home tomorrow to the other side of the world, I wander on this summer's day into the Botanic Gardens, with its giant green-leafed trees and exotic plants exuding their aromatic scents. I find a soft, warm patch of grass beside an old, wise oak tree that shades me from the hot, piercing sun. I look around me. All five senses are brought to life. The clarity of colour, joy, and life in everything I see is like clicking through the slides on an old plastic 3-D View-Master enhancing the world around me—

An azure blue sky and pillow clouds

An energetic brass band playing on the bandstand

People walking arm in arm

Picnics laid out on tartan rugs on the grass

Tea and scones

Biting into a fresh, hard apple

Strongly scented red and yellow roses

Politeness

Smiles to Strangers

Children screaming with laughter

The relaxing sound of the ornate gurgling fountain

Birds chirping in the trees

Light reflecting from the Victorian glasshouse Conservatory

The soft embracing grass beneath me

These simple pleasures and senses are re-energizing my body, mind, and soul, and with a smile, I realize they're simply replicating that feeling of Paradise back at home and helping me get ready for the next unknown journey.

REFLECTION

Travelling out on the road; just you and your wheels.

Through new, lost and isolated places.

Close to home. Far from home.

Riding for hours, days, weeks, months.

The thrill to travel that road and to that place for the first time.

Time to reflect about yourself, what you do in this world and life's purpose.

That undiluted freedom.

The joy to experience new sensations.

That enhanced simplicity of life.

To just come and go as you please.

But ultimately an invisible hand beckons you home.

And you grab it to pull you back.

To a place we know, to where we know we belong.

Where we find happiness.

Some may consider this to be some sort of earthly Paradise.

Zoë Cano—Walton-on-Thames, 2019

Appendix

My Aotearoa New Zealand "Hellbent" Route & Distances

Christchurch to Kaikoura—188 kms

Kaikoura to Picton—211 kms

Picton to Wellington—Ferry plus 8 kms

Wellington to Napier—333 kms

Napier to Rotorua—22 kms

Rotorua to Cooks Beach (Coromandel Peninsula)—229 kms

Cooks Beach to Coromandel—78 kms

Coromandel to Beach Haven, Auckland —192 kms

Auckland to Pakiri Beach—84 kms

Pakiri Beach to Paihia, Bay of Islands—167 kms

Paihia to Ahipara—135 kms

Ahipara to Cape Reinga—198 kms

Ahipara to Orewa—308 kms

Orewa to Raglan—199 kms

Raglan to Whangamomona (through Forgotten World Highway)—312 kms

Whangamomona to Whanganui—202 kms

Whanganui to Paekakariki—190 kms

Paekakariki to Wellington to Rapaura, Marlborough—57 kms

Rapaura to Waipara—264 kms

Waipara to Lake Tekapo ('Starlight Highway')—311 kms

Lake Tekapo to Kakanui—225 kms

Kakanui to Invercargill—343 kms

Invercargill to Te Anau—184 kms

Te Anau to Milford Sound to Te Anau—236 kms

Te Anau to Manapouri to Te Anau—44 kms

Te Anau to Glenorchy—217 kms

Glenorchy to Cardrona, Crown Range—74 kms

Cardrona to Wanaka—24 kms

Wanaka to Oamaru—229 kms

Oamaru to Akaroa—299 kms

Akaroa to Christchurch—82 kms

Note

Exchange rate in February 2018; NZ$ 1 (New Zealand Dollar)=£0.52

References and Reading recommendations

Instructions for New Zealanders by Richard Wolfe

Wild Boy—An Epic Trek around the Coast of New Zealand by Brando Yelavich

Great Tales from Rural New Zealand by Gordon McLauchlan

Excerpts from *To Hahei and Beyond* by Jill Cameron

Lonely Planet's Best of New Zealand

The Rough Guide to New Zealand

Marco Polo Map of New Zealand and Highlights

UNESCO Dark Sky Reserve—

www.earthandsky.co.nz, www.tekapostargazing.co.nz

Travel and road information www.nzta.govt.nz

Accommodation—Airbnb, Hostelworld, BBH Hostels

ACKNOWLEDGEMENTS

Kevin Kinghan, intrepid journalist-come-racer, who generously helped with the Burt Munro Challenge; Sean Wilmot, my Ghost Rider, from *Bike Rider Magazine*, New Zealand; South Pacific Motorcycle Tours for supplying the motorcycle; David Dudfield, Curator of History at the Southland Museum; Jill Cameron, Robyn Lang, Fern Hume, John Tinley, and David Brockington for their insiders' snippets; Hugo Sansome; Andrew Cameron of Palantiri Ltd for the drone photography at the Burt Munro Challenge; Bill Nye of Adventure Books Oamaru; Doctor Mark Smith of the Oamaru Whitestone Civic Trust.

In life we all have dreams. But do we ever attempt to make them happen?

A true story with a difference. She had nothing. No money. No time. No motorbike. No experience for such a mammoth trip. But she did have a clear vision. So with gritted determination, she goes all out to make her dream come true: to travel solo and unassisted across the lesser-known roads of the North American continent covering more than 8,000 km on a classic Triumph Bonneville.

From the outset to the end of this escapade, it's always going to be a question of "Go or Bust" on whether she'll ever succeed or even finish the journey with the most unexpected obstacles, dangers and surprises that come her way. Her wry sense of humour helps without doubt, get her out of some of anyone's worst case scenarios.

An inspiring and motivational story written with passion to succeed against all odds, a true life lesson in believing in yourself— there is no such thing as dreaming too big.

So let the adventure begin!

More from Zoë Cano

Bonneville Go or Bust[1][2] by Zoë Cano
A true story with a difference. Zoë had no experience for such a mammoth adventure of a lifetime but goes all out to make her dream come true to travel solo across the lesser known roads of the American continent on a classic motorcycle.

I loved reading this book. She has a way of putting you right into the scene. It was like riding on the back seat and experiencing this adventure along with Zoë.—★★★★ Amazon Review

Southern Escapades[1][2] by Zoë Cano
As an encore to her cross country trip, Zoë rides along the tropical Gulf of Mexico and Atlantic Coast in Florida, through the forgotten back roads of Alabama and Georgia. This adventure uncovers the many hidden gems of lesser known places in these beautiful Southern states.

. . . Zoë has once again interested and entertained me with her American adventures. Her insightful prose is a delight to read and makes me want to visit the same places.—★★★★★ Amazon Review

Chilli, Skulls & Tequila[1][2] by Zoë Cano
Zoe captures the spirit of beautiful Baja California, Mexico, with a solo 3 000 mile adventure encountering a myriad of surprises along the way and unique, out-of-the-way places tucked into Baja's forgotten corners.

Zoe adds hot chilli and spices to her stories, creating a truly mouth-watering reader's feast!—★★★★★ Waterstones Review

Also from Road Dog Publications

Motorcycles, Life, and . . . [1] [2] **by Brent Allen**
Sit down at a table and talk motorcycles, life and . . . (fill in the blank) with award winning riding instructor and creator of the popular "Howzit Done?" video series, Brent "Capt. Crash" Allen. Here are his thoughts about riding and life and how they combine told in a lighthearted tone.

The Elemental Motorcyclist [1] [2] **by Brent Allen**
Brent's second book offers more insights into life and riding and how they go together. This volume, while still told in the author's typical easy-going tone, gets down to more specifics about being a better rider.

A Short Ride in the Jungle [1] [2] **by Antonia Bolingbroke-Kent**
A young woman tackles the famed Ho Chi Minh Trail alone on a diminutive pink Honda Cub armed only with her love of Southeast Asia, its people, and her wits.

Beads in the Headlight [1] **by Isabel Dyson**
A British couple tackle riding from Alaska to Tierra del Fuego two-up on a 31 year-old BMW "airhead." Join them on this epic journey across two continents.
A great blend of travel, motorcycling, determination, and humor. —★★★★★
Amazon Review

Chasing America [1] [2] **by Tracy Farr**
Tracy Farr sets off on multiple legs of a motorcycle ride to the four corners of America in search of the essence of the land and its people.

In Search of Greener Grass [1] **by Graham Field**
With game show winnings and his KLR 650, Graham sets out solo for Mongolia & beyond. Foreword by Ted Simon

Eureka [1] by Graham Field
Graham sets out on a journey to Kazahkstan only to realize his contrived goal is not making him happy. He has a "Eureka!" moment, turns around, and begins to enjoy the ride as the ride itself becomes the destination.

Different Natures [1] by Graham Field
The story of two early journeys Graham made while living in the US, one north to Alaska and the other south through Mexico. Follow along as Graham tells the stories in his own unique way.

Thoughts on the Road [1] [2] by Michael Fitterling
The Editor of *Vintage Japanese Motorcycle Magazine* ponders his experiences with motorcycles and riding and how they've intersected and influenced his life.

Northeast by Northwest [1] [2] by Michael Fitterling
The author finds two motorcycle journeys of immense help staving off depression and the other effects of stress. Along the way, he discovers the beauty of North America and the kindness of its people.
  . . . one of the most captivating stories I have read in a long time. Truly a MUST read!!—★★★★★ Amazon Review

Hit the Road, Jac! [1] [2] by Jacqui Furneaux
At 50, Jacqui leaves her home and family, buys a motorcycle in India, and begins a seven-year world-wide journey with no particular plan. Along the way she comes to terms with herself and her family.

Asphalt & Dirt [1] [2] by Aaron Heinrich
A compilation of profiles of both famous figures in the motorcycle industry and relatively unknown people who ride, dispelling the myth of the stereotypical "biker" image.

A Tale of Two Dusters & Other Stories [1] [2] by Kirk Swanick
In this collection of tales, Kirk Swanick tells of growing up a gear-head behind both the wheels of muscle cars and the handlebars of motorcycles and describes the joys and trials of riding

Man in the Saddle[12] by Paul van Hoof
Aboard a 1975 Moto Guzzi V7, Paul starts out from Alaska for Ushuaia. Along the way there are many twists and turns, some which change his life forever. English translation from the original Dutch

The Wrong Way Round[12] by Andy Benfield
The tale of the first westerner to cross into Burma from India on a motorcycle in over fifty years. It's also the story of a man coming to grips with his age and his romance with a woman twelve years younger. The story unfolds along some of the world's most stunning landscapes as the couple hurtle toward Burma among the Himalayas.

Those Two Idiots[12] by Jack Grey
Mayhem, mirth, and adventure follow two riders across two continents. Jack and Marcin set off for Thailand thinking they were prepared, more or less, but mostly less. This story if full of mishaps and triumphs told in an amusing self-deprecating style. Here is an honest overland excursion with all the highs and lows, wins and losses, wonderful people and low-lifes, and charms and pitfalls of the countries through which they travel.

Shiny Side Up[12] by Ron Davis
A delightful collection of essays and articles from Ron Davis, Associate Editor and columnist for *BMW Owners News*. This book is filled with tales of the road and recounts the joys and foibles of motorcycle ownership and maintenance. Read it and find out why Ron is a favorite of readers of the *Owners News*!